Decorating with CROCHET

Decorating
with
CROCHET

by
Anne Halliday

Illustrated with Photographs and Diagrams

HOUGHTON MIFFLIN COMPANY
BOSTON, 1975

The photographs in this book are by Guy Sherman
and the charts and diagrams by Bill Meyerriecks.

The design for the Beaded Wall Hanging is used
with permission of Fawcett Publications.

Library of Congress Cataloging in Publication Data

Halliday, Anne.
    Decorating with crochet.

    1. Crocheting.   2. House furnishings.   I. Title.
        TT820.H23   746.9   75-15893
                        ISBN 0-395-20992-7

Printed in the United States of America

K   10 9 8 7 6 5 4 3 2 1

To Louise

Thank you to:

Joanne Whitwell, whose creative and technical assistance
are forever appreciated,

Bill Meyerriecks, illustrator,

Guy Sherman, photographer,

Morton H. Baker, the production manager at Houghton
Mifflin who put it all between two covers,

and

Joyce Hartman, the editor at Houghton Mifflin
who said *yes*.

Contents

Color Illustrations

Introduction

Decorating with Crochet

Not too long ago if you pulled out your crochet in public, people would say "What's that?" and right away you were on the defensive justifying your behavior. Anything that wasn't knitting was immediately suspect and regarded as eccentric.

Today, crocheters are accepted everywhere and the offensive remarks are never more than an occasional "Oh, you're doing that other thing!" Now, at least people are making a distinction.

Crochet was traditionally a lace-making technique and when tastes changed, crochet didn't; it simply grew stale over the years, stagnating in its old-fashioned image — the stepchild of the needle arts. But with the advent of the needlework revival, a lot of new talent and creative designing finally pushed crochet out of the Victorian parlor and into the twentieth century. The clothing fads of the sixties started a whole new wave of crochet enthusiasm, revamping the old familiar doilies into cloche hats, afghans into sweaters, and potholders into pullovers.

Crochet flourished on the fashion scene, but what's been happening on the home front? There's a lot of stitching going on but crochet still isn't a household word and has yet to attain the artistic status enjoyed by its competitive crafts. We've been inundated with needlepoint from seat covers to book covers, weaving has warped and weft us beautiful rugs and tapestries, macramé planters are climbing the walls, and our sofas are sagging under voluminous mounds of embroidered pillows. But where are their crochet counterparts?

Occasionally you do see some interesting home accessories scattered among the needlework magazines, but most designs lack the zest and excitement current with our contemporary lifestyles. Crochet is so much more than the repetitious fare of afghans and potholders; its artistic potential has been virtually untapped.

Crochet is unique. The inherent characteristics of the stitches and patterns create a versatile medium that can cleverly simulate other stitchery forms. Tapestries are traditionally woven on a loom, but they can also be crocheted; cotton cords and wood beads can be whipped up into macramé-style plant hangers; unusual rug textures are possible, many of which can *only* be created with a crochet hook; seat cushions and other furniture treatments can be stitched to imitate needlepoint; and crocheted appliqués strike a similarity to crewel embroidery.

Decorating with crochet is a natural extension of the unlimited possibilities this special craft offers. Interior decorating has become a popular pastime, and more and more people are taking the do-it-yourself route, not only to save money, but to satisfy that creative urge for self-expression. Our homes reflect our individual tastes and preferences, and what can better express our personal likes than those things we make ourselves? A sofa and a couple of chairs can make a living room, but it's the extra touches that make it a room to live in — decorating spice that adds a flavor uniquely your own. Furniture is the functional side of living; the extra touches humanize the practical.

A craft with such a challenging future just had to be explored. As an ardent crocheter and needlecraft designer, I was irresistibly drawn to that challenge, which has culminated in the ideas set forth in this book. Here is a collection of designs with instructions to stir the imagination of crochet fans who want to try a different approach to home decorating. This is by no means a decorating guide, but rather an eye opener to unusual projects that you can make for your home — crocheted treasures to live with and enjoy for years to come.

Quality of Materials

Never before have the fiber industries so saturated the needlework market. Yarns are available in every conceivable fiber, texture, color, ply, and twist, and drug stores to supermarkets are setting up bargain yarn displays alongside toothpaste and canned soups to lure in hungry needlecraft consumers. However, these bargain yarns usually reflect the reality in that old truism — you get what you pay for.

There is no substitute for quality. If you are willing to dedicate the time and energy to handmade projects, why not start out with materials that will last? The longest-lasting yarns are those made with the natural fibers of wool, linen, or cotton. They have a built-in resistance to wear and keep their fresh look over many years.

There are also many fine acrylic yarns that handle and wear almost as well as the natural fibers, but since the significant increase in wool prices, a lot of inferior off-brand acrylic "wools" are being packaged under snappy labels with catchy price tags and promoted as big money-savers. You save nothing. These bargain yarns are usually lifeless, dull, and stringy, and are simply pulling the wool, or nonwool if you will, over too many consumer's eyes. When buying yarn, stick to the established brands that reflect the integrity and carry the guarantee of experienced manufacturers.

General Information

The materials for the projects in this book were selected for quality and practical use. All the items can be either washed or dry-cleaned and most pillows are designed with removable covers. Cleaning information is given at the end of each set of directions.

Under the "Materials" heading at the beginning of each instruction, the yarn brand and colors given are those used to make the photographed sample. If another yarn will work equally as well, the alternate is listed afterward. However, when alternate materials are given, it doesn't necessarily follow that the substitute yarn is available in the same colors or quantities; and the specific colors mentioned should not preclude your choosing your own color combinations. Please do. Personal taste and color schemes vary; so of course coordinate according to your own needs.

Before starting a project, it's a good idea to skim over the directions in order to acquaint yourself with the work sequence and the materials you'll need. Often additional materials are listed for mounting or assembly that might otherwise be overlooked.

Be sure to read the introductory remarks preceding each set of instructions. In many cases they contain pertinent information not covered in the actual directions.

All the projects are worked with the basic crochet method. Gadget-related crochet, such as hairpin lace, broomstick lace, daisies, and afghan stitch, has been avoided because of the additional techniques involved.

The Appendix starts on p. 139. Look it over before you begin work. It contains a good deal of helpful information that is better known before than after.

A Note on Supplies

The materials used for the projects were available at the time of writing and, to the best of my knowledge, will continue to be available. But manufacturers update their lines, adding new yarns and discarding others; so it's possible that some materials or colors may eventually be discontinued.

Don't panic if you can't find the color you want or if a particular yarn is no longer carried. In many cases a manufacturer will have a similar yarn that can be substituted, or your local needlecraft shop may be able to suggest an alternate by another manufacturer.

On p. 152 in the Appendix is a list of the names and addresses of all the manufacturers whose materials are used. If you have any problem finding supplies in your area, write directly to the manufacturers for information. All materials are nationally distributed; so they will be able to provide you with the names of the nearest dealers carrying their products. Some manufacturers, as noted, will sell direct to the consumer.

THE DESIGNS

1. Tapestries

Perhaps the artistry of crochet is best demonstrated with tapestries. A good design plus careful selection of materials can produce an exceptional piece of work worthy of its tapestry status.

The tapestries are all worked in the jacquard crochet technique, which is a method of changing yarn colors to reproduce a crocheted design or picture from a chart — worked in either double crochet or single crochet stitches. Starting on p. 145 in the Appendix, you will find detailed instructions for both stitch techniques.

The yarn used is Reynolds Icelandic Lopi Wool, one of the most beautiful and unusual yarns available. Its heavy texture gives about three stitches to the inch; so the work goes fairly quickly. Any bulky wool yarn can be used, but select your materials wisely. Don't skimp on quality.

All the tapestries are designed to hang on a café curtain rod, which can either be mounted on the wall with accompanying brackets or suspended on chains from ceiling hooks.

Tapestries also make intriguing room dividers when backed with an appropriate fabric. Or if you're doubly ambitious, work a second tapestry using another design charted with the same number of stitches and rows as the first (eliminating the turn-under allowance), and join them back to back with a simple crocheted edging.

Eagle Tapestry

Color Photograph, p. 6

Throughout civilization, man has always attached a special significance to birds. The concept of avian veneration — most likely inspired by the mystery of flight — has often stimulated a curious dig into the past. Having shared ten years of my life with a precocious parrot, I have spent many hours wondering over this unique attraction of man and bird.

The Egyptians worshiped Horus, the falcon-headed god of light and heaven, and gave the long-legged ibis sacred status and free run of the Nile. The Greek god Zeus wooed his lady love, Leda, in the guise of a swan. And Nike, the goddess of victory, stands headless but immortal in the Louvre, her alabaster feathers outstretched, as the Winged Victory of Samothrace.

When the Roman legions returned from battle, the standard-bearers triumphantly led the march of conquering heroes with bannered stanchions crested with the noble eagle. The

Germans and the Russians liked the eagle too — with two heads. And of course, our very own bald eagle has become — along with apple pie — the symbol of all things American.

English and French architecture is copiously gargoyled with fantastical birdlike creatures perched aloft Gothic gables. And in heraldry, birds have been used for centuries to distinguish the Baileys from the Bartletts.

The thunderbird reigned supreme atop the American Indian totem and the Incas attributed secret powers to the condor. The dove marked the end of the Great Flood and, since Noah's ark, has remained the universal symbol of peace. The albatross means good luck to sailors and the gull has long been the seafarer's fair-weather guide. Air mail started with the carrier pigeon, and certainly all inspiration for the incredible feats of aviation — from Icarus to Lindbergh — was born from the wings of birds.

But of all the birds, it is the eagle that stands the noblest. Its solitary, monogamous life, centered around a hidden and lofty aerie, suggests an independence unique among the more gregarious nature of most birds. With no natural enemies to challenge its survival (discounting man's intervention), the eagle is virtually unconquerable. And from its powerful mien emanate the strength and majestic dignity for which it is emblematic.

The bold color definition and strong lines of the tapestry design combine to convey these qualities in a stitchery tribute to the eagle. The tapestry is worked in the double crochet jacquard technique and finished off with a braided fringe across the lower edge.

FINISHED SIZE: Approx. 32″ × 52″ plus 10″ fringe

MATERIALS:
   Reynolds Icelandic Lopi Wool (3.6 oz. skeins):
     1 skein White #51
     2 skeins Turquoise #73
     3 skeins each of Lt. Brown #65 and Natural
       Black #52
     5 skeins Lt. Gray #56
   Crochet Hook Size H
   Tapestry Needle #13
   Café Curtain Rod — extendable from 28″ to 48″
   Wall Brackets or Hooks and Chain for hanging

GAUGE: 3 dc = 1 inch
         2 rows = 1¼ inches

NOTE: Before starting, refer to p. 145 for instructions on how to work jacquard crochet. Eagle is worked with double crochet method. Each square on chart = 2 dc.

To Start — Row 1 (Wrong Side): With Lt. Brown, ch 106, work 1 dc in 4th ch from hook and in each ch across — 104 dc counting beginning ch-3 as 1 dc.

Row 2: Turn — right side, sl st in first dc, ch 2 — counts as first dc (*Note: For an even edge, always work turning ch in this manner*), work 1 dc in each dc across working last dc in top of end ch. Follow chart for remainder of tapestry. Pattern starts with Row 3 on wrong side of work.

Finishing: Thread Lt. Gray on tapestry needle. On each long side, turning first 2 sts of edge to wrong side, sew edge to back with overcast stitch working in top surface of back sts. At top, sewing with Turquoise yarn, turn first 2 rows to wrong side and stitch same as long sides. Leave ends open.

Fringe: (*Note: See p. 142 for instructions on knotting fringe.*) Cut a 28″ length of Lt. Gray for each fringe. Knot 1 fringe in single loop of each ch across lower edge for total of 100 fringes. Attach an additional *single strand* about 18″ long to last ch at one end so that strand hangs evenly with other fringes. Weave remaining short end of strand through sts on wrong side. Braiding: With right side facing, start at left side and plait first 3 *strands* like a pigtail to within 1½″ from end, turn braid over itself and make a knot, trim ends evenly leaving 1″ of yarn below knot. Plaiting next 3 strands, braid remainder of fringe the same.

Blocking: See p. 141 for blocking instructions.

3

ROW 3: START PATTERN (WRONG SIDE)

- ⬜ LIGHT BROWN
- ⬛ TURQUOISE
- ⬛ NATURAL BLACK
- ⬜ WHITE
- ⬜ LIGHT GRAY

To Hang: Insert rod through top tunnel, extending rod about 2″ from each end. Mount wall brackets or hooks to correspond, and hang.

Cleaning: Have dry-cleaned. See p. 142 for dry cleaning information.

Medieval Bird

Color Photograph, p. 7

The design for this unlikely bird was adapted from an authentic *"drôlerie"* taken from an illuminated manuscript of the Apocalypse of St. John — the book of the Bible most frequently used for pictorial illustrations during the Middle Ages. *Drôleries* are the line drawings of animals and fantastic creatures found in the margins of these manuscripts, conjured from the quaint imagination of the scribe who did the lettering.

The bird is worked in the single crochet jacquard technique and framed in a striped border that repeats the colors of the bird. Brass rings are crocheted into the top edge for hanging.

FINISHED SIZE: Approx. 25½″ × 25½″ including border

MATERIALS:

Reynolds Icelandic Lopi Wool (3.6 oz. skeins):
1 skein each of Orange #71, Yellow #61, and Turquoise #73
3 skeins White #51
Crochet Hook Size H
Tapestry Needle #13
14 Brass Rings — 1⅛″ outside diam.
Café Curtain Rod — extendable from 28″ to 48″

Wall Brackets or Hooks and Chain for hanging

GAUGE: 3 sc = 1 inch
7 rows = 2 inches

NOTE: Before starting, refer to p. 145 for instructions on how to work jacquard crochet. Bird is worked with single crochet method. Each square on chart = 1 sc.

To Start — Row 1 (Wrong Side): With White, ch 71, work 1 sc in 2nd ch from hook and in each ch across — 70 sc.

ROW 12: START PATTERN (RIGHT SIDE)

☐ YELLOW ■ ORANGE ■ TURQUOISE ☐ WHITE

8

Row 2: Ch 1, turn — right side, work 1 sc in each sc across.

Follow chart for remainder of tapestry. Pattern starts with Row 12 on right side of work.

Border

Note: All rnds are worked from right side. On lower edge, work in single loop of ch sts.

Rnd 1 — Lower Edge: With right side facing and starting on lower edge with Orange, insert hook in 5th ch from left corner, yo and draw up a loop, sl st in next 4 ch sts, mark last sl st made — corner.

First Side: Working along edge of rows, sl st in between the last 2 sc of rows as follows: sl st in next 6 rows, * sk 1 row, sl st in next 6 rows; repeat from * across, end with 7 sl sts — 67 sl sts made after last marked st.

Top Edge: Sl st in first sc, mark sl st just made, sl st in each sc across top, mark last sl st made — 68 sl sts between marked sts.

Second Side: Work same as First Side.

Remainder of Lower Edge: Sl st in first ch, mark sl st just made, sl st in each ch across, end with sl st in same ch as start — 68 sl sts between marked sts, join with sl st to *back loop* of first sl st. *Do not break yarn.*

Rnd 2: Working in *back loop* of each st, work 1 sc in each sl st around working 3 sc in marked sl sts, remove markers as each corner is worked, join with sl st to *both loops* of first sc. Fasten off.

Note: Work in both loops of each st for remainder of border. See p. 141 for helpful hint on working over joinings.

Rnd 3: Starting at a place away from last join, from right side attach Yellow in any st as follows: holding yarn at back of work, yo hook, then insert hook in st and under end of yarn, yo and draw up a loop, yo and through both loops on hook — sc made, work 1 sc in each sc around working 3 sc in center sc at each corner, join with sl st to first sc. Fasten off.

Repeat Rnd 3 three times in the following color sequence: Turquoise, Yellow, and Orange. *Do not break yarn after last rnd.*

Edging: Ch 1, do not turn, work 1 sc in same sc as join, work in reverse sc as follows: * *working toward the right,* ch 1, sk next sc, insert hook in next sc, *hook over yarn* and draw up a loop, yo and through both loops on hook — sc made; repeat from * around ending in st just before corner of top edge, ch 1, sk next sc, attach ring as follows: insert hook in next sc, place ring over hook, *hook over yarn* and draw up a loop, yo and through both loops on hook; continue edging across top, attaching a ring in every 3rd sc ending with ring at next corner; continue edging around remaining sides, join to first sc drawing yarn through to wrong side. Fasten off.

Blocking: See p. 141 for blocking instructions.

To Hang: Insert rod through rings, extending rod about 2″ from each end. Mount wall brackets or hooks to correspond, and hang.

Cleaning: Have dry-cleaned. See p. 142 for dry cleaning information.

Grandfather Clock

Color Photograph, p. 14

A grandfather clock where time stands mysteriously still between the hours! All the character and charm of its old-fashioned predecessor are captured in a stylized wall hanging stitched in the double crochet jacquard technique. It may not be the ultimate in precision clockwork, but its life-size realism makes an amusing surprise at the head of the stairs, or in a hallway or foyer.

FINISHED SIZE: Approx. 21″ × 68″

MATERIALS:

Reynolds Icelandic Lopi Wool (3.6 oz. skeins):
   2 skeins each of White #51 and Dk. Brown #66
   3 skeins each of Natural Black #52 and Lt. Brown #65
   5 skeins Lt. Gray #56
Crochet Hook Size H
Tapestry Needle #13
Café Curtain Rod — extendable from 16″ to 28″
Wall Brackets or Hooks and Chain for hanging

GAUGE: 3 dc = 1 inch
         2 rows = 1¼ inches

NOTE: Before starting, refer to p. 145 for instructions on how to work jacquard crochet. Clock is worked with double crochet method. Each square on chart = 2 dc.

To Start — Row 1 (Wrong Side): With Lt. Gray, ch 72, work 1 dc in 4th ch from hook and in each ch across — 70 dc counting beginning ch-3 as first dc.

Row 2: Turn — right side, sl st in first dc, ch 2 — counts as first dc (*Note: For an even edge, always work turning ch in this manner*), work 1 dc in each dc across working last dc in top of end ch.
Follow chart for remainder of tapestry. Pattern starts with Row 4 on right side of work.

Finishing: Thread Lt. Gray on tapestry needle. On each long side, turning first 2 sts of edge to wrong side, sew edge to back with overcast stitch working in top surface of back sts. At top and bottom, turn first 2 rows to wrong side and stitch same as long sides. Leave ends open.

Blocking: See p. 141 for blocking instructions.

To Hang: Insert rod through top tunnel, extending rod about 2″ from each end. Mount wall brackets or hooks to correspond, and hang.

Cleaning: Have dry-cleaned. See p. 142 for dry cleaning information.

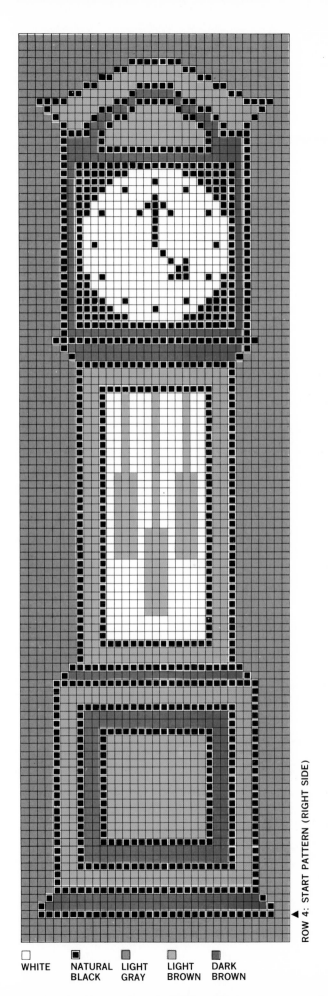

◄ ROW 4: START PATTERN (RIGHT SIDE)

☐ WHITE ■ NATURAL BLACK ▨ LIGHT GRAY ▨ LIGHT BROWN ▨ DARK BROWN

2. Area Rugs

The versatility of area rugs makes them a favorite in floor décor. They work on wood floors, stone floors, tile floors, or over carpet, and their small size is an easy fit in tight spots such as foyers, dens, hallways, and stair landings.

A single rug can be the focal point of a room or several can coordinate a series of furniture groupings. They can be changed around when the mood moves you and they're convenient to clean. Directions for five rugs are given on the following pages, each a different example of the unique textures that only crochet can produce.

As a precautionary note: rugs placed directly on bare wood floors can be slippery and dangerous. I would suggest placing a thin, rubber mat underneath to prevent sliding. The mat can be purchased inexpensively at a rug and carpet store; either have the store cut it or cut it yourself slightly smaller than the rug dimensions so that it doesn't show along the edges. For rugs with an open pattern, stick carpet tape (a heavy-duty double-faced tape) on the back of the solid areas to hold it in place.

Irish Crochet Rug

Color Photograph, p. 15

What better complements a country bedroom than an Irish crochet rug? Its old-fashioned lacy elegance blends in beautifully with oaken chests and bare wood floors. It's made with Reynolds Tapis Pingouin rug yarn, a French acrylic that rivals the wool off a sheep's back for resiliency and texture. Don't let the rug's five-foot diameter fool you; the work goes quickly and you could have it finished in a diligent weekend.

SIZE: Approx. 5′ in diam. including 4″ fringe

MATERIALS:
Reynolds Tapis Pingouin Rug Yarn (1¾ oz. skeins):
  34 skeins White #05
Alternate: Any equivalent weight bulky rug yarn
Crochet Hook Size J
Jumbo Crochet Hook Size Q (for working braid only)

NOTE: All rnds are worked from right side.

Rnd 1 (Right Side): With J Hook, ch 1 loosely for center, ch 1 more, work 10 sc in center ch, join with sl st to first sc.

Rnd 2: Ch 3 — counts as first dc, 1 dc in same sc as join, * 2 dc in next sc; repeat from * around, join with sl st to top of ch-3 — 20 dc. Fasten off. (Circle measures about 3½″ in diam.)

Note: Rnds 3–6 are each started with a new strand to avoid making seam. Attach each strand away from join of previous rnd. See helpful hint on p. 141 for working over joinings.

Rnd 3: Attach new strand away from last join as follows: holding yarn at back of work, yo hook, then from right side insert hook in any st and under end of yarn, yo and draw up a loop, yo and through both loops on hook — sc made (*Note: Attach all new strands in this manner*), ch 3 — sc plus ch-3 count as first dc and first ch-1 space, 1 dc in next dc, * ch 1, 1 dc in next dc; repeat from * around ending with ch-1, join with sl st to 2nd ch at start — 20 dc and 20 spaces. Fasten off.

Rnd 4: Attach new strand in any dc — sc made, ch 2 (sc plus ch-2 count as first dc), work 1 dc in each space and each dc around, join with sl st to top of ch-2 — 40 dc. Fasten off.

Rnd 5: Attach new strand in any dc — sc made, ch 3 (sc plus ch-3 count as first tr), 1 tr in same dc, * 1 tr in each of next 3 dc, 2 tr in next dc, 1 tr in each of next 4 dc, 2 tr in next dc; repeat from * around ending with 1 tr in each of last 4 dc, join with sl st to top of ch-3 — 55 tr. Fasten off.

Rnd 6: Attach new strand in any tr — sc made, ch 3 (sc plus ch-3 count as first tr), 1 tr in same tr, * (1 tr in each of next 2 tr, 2 tr in next tr) 3 times, 1 tr in each of next 3 tr, 2 tr in next tr; repeat from * around ending in 3rd tr from start, 1 tr in each of next 2 tr, join with sl st to top of ch-3 — 72 tr. *Do not break yarn.* (Circle measures about 12½″ in diam.)

Rnd 7: Ch 1, 1 sc in top of ch-3 of last rnd, * ch 3, sl st in sc working in the 2 *side* loops of st — picot, ch 4, sk 2 tr, 1 sc in next tr; repeat from * around ending with picot in 3rd tr from start, ch 2, join by working 1 dc in first sc — 24 loops.

Rnd 8: Ch 3, sl st in top of joining-st of last rnd — picot, * ch 5, 1 sc over center of next loop, work picot; repeat from * around, ch 2, join by working 1 tr in base of first picot.

Rnd 9: Repeat Rnd 8.

Rnd 10: Ch 3, sl st in top of joining-st of last rnd — picot, * ch 6, 1 sc over next loop, work picot; repeat from * around, ch 3, join by working 1 tr in base of first picot.

Rnd 11: * Ch 5, 1 sc over next loop; repeat from * around ending with ch-5, join with sl st to top of joining-st of last rnd.

Rnd 12: Ch 4 — counts as first tr, work 1 tr in each ch and each sc around, join with sl st to top of ch-4 — 144 tr. (Circle measures about 23″ in diam.)

Rnd 13: Ch 5 — counts as first dc and first ch-2 space, sk 1 tr, 1 dc in next tr, * ch 1, sk 1 tr, 1 dc in next tr, ch 2, sk 1 tr, 1 dc in next tr; repeat from * around ending with ch-1, sk next tr, join with sl st to 3rd ch at start — 72 spaces.

Rnd 14: Ch 5 — counts as first dtr, work 1 dtr (yo 3 times) in each ch st and each dc around, join with sl st to top of ch-5 — 180 dtr. Drop work temporarily. Place last loop on safety pin to hold while working braid.

Braid: The braid is formed by slip stitching over the double crochet stitches of Rnd 13. Using 4 new skeins, work with 4 strands of yarn held together as one strand. Use an even tension to keep braid as elastic as rest of work. Holding yarn at back of work, from right side insert Q Hook in any space, yo at back and draw up a loop through space, * working toward left, insert hook in next space, yo hook at back and draw up a loop through space and then through loop on hook — sl st made; repeat from * around ending in last space just before starting space. To finish off ends: cut yarn leaving strands 12″ long, pull ends out through last sl st to front; insert hook *under* the top 2 loops of *first* sl st made and pull yarn ends through loops out to one side; from wrong side insert hook *between* the top 2 loops of *last* sl st made and draw yarn to wrong side. Fasten off by weaving beginning and end strands through dc's on wrong side. Reserve remainder of skeins for 2nd round of braid.

Rnd 15: Pick up dropped loop and continue, ch 1,

16

1 sc in top of ch-5 of last rnd, * work picot, ch 4, sk 2 dtr, 1 sc in next dtr; repeat from * around ending with picot in 3rd dtr from start, ch 2, join by working 1 dc in base of first picot — 60 loops.

Rnds 16–18: Repeat Rnd 8 three times.

Rnds 19–24: Repeat Rnd 10 six times.

Rnd 25: Repeat Rnd 11.

Rnd 26: Repeat Rnd 12 — 360 tr.

Rnd 27: Ch 5 — counts as first dc and first ch-2 space, sk 1 tr, 1 dc in next tr, * ch 2, sk 1 tr, 1 dc in next tr; repeat from * around ending with ch-2, sk next tr, join with sl st to 3rd ch at start — 180 spaces. Fasten off. Work braid over dc's of Rnd 27 as before.

Fringe: (*Note: See p. 142 for instructions on knotting fringe.*) Wrap yarn around a piece of cardboard 5½″ wide, cut yarn at one edge; combine 4 strands for 1 fringe and knot a fringe in each ch-2 space of last rnd next to braid; trim evenly.

Blocking: See p. 141 for blocking instructions.

Cleaning: The rug can be washed in the washing machine and laid out to dry if you've got the room. The yarn does not retain much moisture so it dries quickly, but I would suggest laying it over large sheets of paper or plastic to protect the surface underneath. The only drawback to washing is that the plies of the fringe tend to untwist and become rather fuzzy. This isn't necessarily a drawback but something you should keep in mind. The effect is very becoming. Some people purposefully brush out fringe to get the same look.

Wash in an automatic washer that spins semi-dry. The rug should never be put through a wringer. Use cold or lukewarm water with soap powder or flakes. Do not use strong detergent. Do not put in drier. To dry, lay out flat, away from sun or heat. Let dry thoroughly before removing.

If you want the rug to retain its original appearance, have it dry-cleaned. The fringe goes through the chemical process without fraying. See p. 142 for dry cleaning information.

Geometric Rug

Color Photograph, p. 22

Three dozen triangles make up the geometry in this giant 4½-foot star. If you've got a super-large bathroom, it makes a wild bathmat. If you've got a young child, it makes playing on the floor more fun. If you don't have either, make it for somebody who does.

SIZE: Approx. 50″ at widest spread plus 4″ tassels

MATERIALS:
  Reynolds Bulky Reynelle (2 oz. skeins):
    5 skeins each of Royal Blue, Lemon Yellow, Scarlet Red, and Kelly Green
    4 skeins Natural White
  Alternate: Bucilla Multi-Craft Yarn or any equivalent weight bulky yarn
  Crochet Hook Size H
  Tapestry Needle #13

GAUGE: 3 sc = 1 inch
    4 rows = 1¼ inches
    Each triangle is approx.
    6″ × 10″ × 11½″

NOTE: Do not remove markers until indicated.

First Triangle (Make 9 Kelly Green and 9 Lemon Yellow)
Row 1: Ch 19, work 1 sc in 2nd ch from hook and in each ch across — 18 sc.
Row 2: Ch 1, turn — right side, dec as follows: insert hook in first sc and draw up a loop, insert hook in next sc and draw up a loop, yo and through all 3 loops on hook, work 1 sc in each sc across.
Row 3: Ch 1, turn, 1 sc in each sc across.
Repeat Rows 2 & 3 until 1 st remains ending with Row 2 — 34 rows. Fasten off.

Border — First Triangle
Note: On short end work in single loop of foundation chain.
Starting on short end with Natural White, from right side insert hook in first ch at right corner, yo and draw up a loop, sl st in each ch across, mark last sl st made — corner; working along edge of rows, sl st in between the last 2 sc of each row across, sl st in top of sc at point, mark sl st just made — 33 sts between marked sts; working across next side, sk first row, sl st in each of next 3 rows, * sk next row, sl st in each of next 4 rows; repeat from * across, sl st in starting ch, mark sl st just made — 27 sts between last 2 marked sts and 16 sts between marked sts on short end. Fasten off.

Second Triangle (Make 9 Royal Blue and 9 Scarlet Red)
Row 1: Work same as First Triangle.
Row 2: Ch 1, turn — right side, 1 sc in each sc across to within 2 sts from end, dec over last 2 sts.
Row 3: Ch 1, turn, 1 sc in each sc across.
Repeat Rows 2 & 3 until 1 st remains ending with Row 2 — 34 rows. Fasten off.

Border — Second Triangle
Starting on short end with Natural White, from right side insert hook in first ch at right corner, yo and draw up a loop, sl st in each ch across, mark last sl st made — corner; working along edge of rows, sl st in between the last 2 sc of each of next 3 rows, * sk next row, sl st in each of next 4 rows; repeat from * across, sl st in top of sc at point, mark sl st just made — 27 sts between marked sts; working across next side, sk first row, sl st in next row and in each row across, sl st in starting ch, mark sl st just made — 33 sts between last 2 marked sts and 16 sts between marked sts on short end. Fasten off.

Assembly
Note: Triangles are sewn together. Refer to Assembly and Color Placement Diagrams. See p. 143 for overcast stitch diagram.
Join First Rnd of Triangles: Place 2 triangles side by side with right sides up. With Natural White and tapestry needle, sew in overcast stitch working in *both loops* of all sl sts. Start sewing in marked st at top point and end in marked st at next corner. Use a separate strand of yarn for each seam.
Center Circle — Rnd 1 (Right Side): With Natural White, ch 2, work 8 sc in center ch, join with sl st to first sc.
Rnd 2: Ch 2 — counts as first hdc, do not turn, work 2 hdc in same sc as join, work 3 hdc in each sc around, join with sl st to top of ch-2 — 24 hdc. Fasten off.
Sew Center Circle in place same as triangles: Match 1 st on circle to each marked sl st at point of triangles and each seam between points. As you sew, remove markers from triangles at *top points only.*
Join Second Rnd of Triangles: Join 2 triangles to form 1 large triangle. Then sew base of each triangle to base of triangles on first rnd; start and end sewing in marked sts at corners. As you sew, remove markers from *center of base only.*
Join Third Rnd of Triangles: Join long sides of 2 triangles, then sew each section to "V" formed by 2nd rnd; start sewing at center of "V" matching marked sts, and sew across short end to next marked st; sew other end the same. A space will

be formed at center of "V." Remove remaining markers as you sew.

Small Circles (Make 6): With Natural White, ch 2, work 6 sc in 2nd ch from hook, join with sl st to first sc. Fasten off.

Sew a Small Circle in each space at center of "V," matching 1 st of circle to 1 seam plus 1 sl st at corner of triangle.

Edging: With Natural White, sl st in *back loop only* of each sl st around entire outer edge.

Tassels (Make 4 each of Royal Blue, Lemon Yellow, Kelly Green, and Scarlet Red): Wrap yarn around a 4″ piece of cardboard 18 times and make tassels according to instructions on p. 142. Arrange tassels according to Color Placement Diagram.

Blocking: See p. 141 for blocking instructions.

Cleaning: Rug can be washed, but because of its size, dry cleaning is recommended. See p. 142 for dry cleaning information.

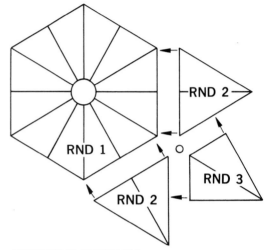

ASSEMBLY DIAGRAM

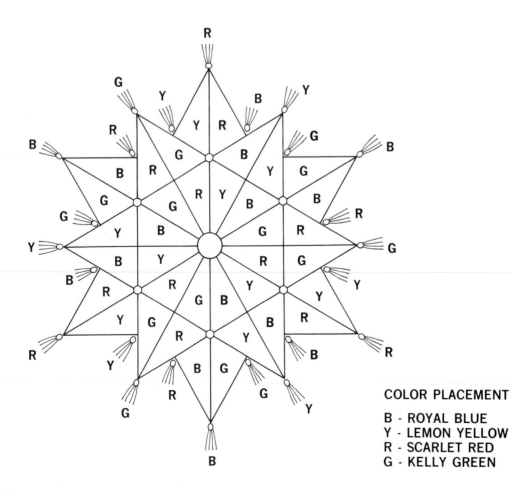

COLOR PLACEMENT

B - ROYAL BLUE
Y - LEMON YELLOW
R - SCARLET RED
G - KELLY GREEN

20

Granny Squares Rug

Color Photograph, p. 22

Granny squares are practical, portable, fast, fun, and forever — and never seem to run short on creative variations. These are sewn together in a square, then bordered with more rows of the same colors to make a 3½-foot rug. Of course, if you want, you can make it larger by adding more squares or shape it as a rectangle. Any way you choose, it makes a charming footwarmer.

SIZE: Approx. 36″ × 36″ plus 4″ fringe

MATERIALS:
Reynolds Tapis Pingouin Rug Yarn (1¾ oz. skeins):
  6 skeins Pink #8, 9 skeins Rose #10, and 15 skeins Dk. Blue #15
Alternate: Any equivalent weight bulky rug yarn
Crochet Hook Size I
Tapestry Needle #13

GAUGE: Each motif is a 10″ square

Motif (Make 9)
Row 1 (Right Side): With Pink, ch 1 loosely for center, ch 1 more, work 8 sc in center ch, join with sl st to first sc.
Row 2: Ch 1, do not turn, work 1 sc, ch 2, 1 sc all in same sc as join — corner, * ch 1, sk next sc, work 1 sc, ch 2, 1 sc all in next sc — corner; repeat from * twice, ch 1, sk next sc, join with sl st to first sc. Fasten off.
Row 3: Turn — wrong side, attach Rose in any corner space as follows: holding yarn at back of work, yo hook, then insert hook in space and under end of yarn, yo and draw up a loop, yo and through both loops on hook — sc made (*Note: Attach all new strands in this manner*), ch 2, 1 sc in same space, * ch 1, 1 sc in next ch-1 space, ch 1, work 1 sc, ch 2, 1 sc all in next corner space; repeat from * twice, ch 1, 1 sc in next ch-1 space, ch 1, join with sl st to first sc. *Do not break yarn.*
Row 4: Ch 1, turn — right side, * (1 sc in next ch-1 space, ch 1) twice, work 1 sc, ch 2, 1 sc all in next corner space, ch 1; repeat from * 3 times, join with sl st to first sc. Fasten off.
Row 5: Turn — wrong side, attach Dk. Blue in any corner space — sc made, ch 2, 1 sc in same space, ** * ch 1, 1 sc in next ch-1 space * ; repeat from * to * across ending in last space before corner, ch 1, work 1 sc, ch 2, 1 sc all in corner space; repeat from ** twice; repeat from * to * across ending in last space before start, ch 1, join with sl st to first sc. *Do not break yarn.*

Row 6: Ch 1, turn — right side, 1 sc in next ch-1 space, ** * ch 1, 1 sc in next ch-1 space * ; repeat from * to * across ending in last space before corner; ch 1, work 1 sc, ch 2, 1 sc all in corner space; repeat from ** 3 times, ch 1, join with sl st to first sc. Fasten off.
Repeat Rows 5 & 6 three times in the following color sequence: 2 rows each of Pink, Rose, and Dk. Blue; *on last Dk. Blue row work 3 ch sts between sc's in each corner space.*

Assembly: With tapestry needle and Dk. Blue, sew motifs together in a square with 3 rows of 3 motifs each. Sew from right side with overcast stitch (see p. 143 for overcast stitch diagram), inserting needle through *back loop only* of each sc and each ch. Start sewing in center ch of one corner and end in center ch of next corner. Sew with an even tension to keep seam as elastic as motifs.

Border — Row 1: From wrong side attach Dk. Blue in any corner space of rug — sc made, ch 2, 1 sc in same space, * ch 1, 1 sc in next space * ; repeat from * to * 10 times, ** ch 1, 1 sc in corner space of same motif, ch 1, sk seam, 1 sc in corner space of next motif; repeat from * to * 11 times; repeat from ** once, ch 1, work 1 sc, ch 2, 1 sc all in corner space, continue around remaining sides in the same manner ending with ch-1, join with sl st to first sc. *Do not break yarn.*
Row 2: Repeat Row 6 of Motif.
Repeat Rows 5 & 6 of Motif for 6 more rows in the following color sequence: 2 rows each of Pink, Rose, and Dk. Blue.

Fringe: (*Note: See p. 142 for instructions on knotting fringe.*) Wrap Dk. Blue around a piece of cardboard 5½″ wide; cut yarn at one side. Combine 2 strands for 1 fringe and knot a fringe in each space around all sides; trim evenly.

Blocking: See p. 141 for blocking instructions.

Cleaning: See cleaning instructions for Irish Crochet Rug on p. 17.

Reversible Rug

Color Photograph, p. 23

Another granny squares rug — this time with a different twist. While one side shows off a series of woven squares outlined in raised borders, the reverse side is flat and patterned with a ridged texture. Either way, it makes a perfect bedside warmer or a cozy sitting spot in front of the fire.

SIZE: Approx. 36″ × 54″ plus 3″ fringe

MATERIALS:
   Reynolds Bulky Reynelle (2 oz. skeins):
     29 skeins Natural #9514
   Alternate: Bucilla Multi-Craft yarn or any equiv-
     alent weight bulky yarn
   Crochet Hook Size J

GAUGE: Each motif is a 9″ square

NOTE: All rnds are worked from front side. Weave in yarn ends so that they are invisible from both sides.

Motif (Make 24)
Rnd 1 — Front Side: Ch 1 loosely for center, ch 3

more, work 15 dc in center ch, join with sl st to 3rd ch at start — 16 dc counting ch-3 as first dc.

Rnd 2: Ch 6, 1 dc in top of ch-3, work 1 long dc around post of next dc as follows: yo, insert hook under post of next dc bringing hook out on left side of post to front of work, yo and draw up a ¾" loop, (yo and through 2 loops on hook) twice, work 1 long dc around each post of next 2 dc, * work 1 regular dc, ch 3, 1 regular dc all in next dc — corner (*Note: All dc's worked in corners are regular dc's*), work 1 long dc around each post of next 3 dc; repeat from * twice, join with sl st to 3rd ch at start — 5 dc on each side.

Rnd 3: Sl st in next corner space, ch 3 — always counts as first dc, work 1 dc, ch 3, 2 dc all in same space, work 1 long dc around each post of next 5 dc, * work 2 dc, ch 3, 2 dc all in next space, work 1 long dc around each post of next 5 dc; repeat from * twice, join with sl st to 3rd ch at start — 9 dc on each side.

Rnd 4: Sl st in next dc and in corner space, ch 3, work 1 dc, ch 3, 2 dc all in same space, work 1 long dc around post of each dc to next corner, * work 2 dc, ch 3, 2 dc all in corner space, work 1 long dc around post of each dc to next corner; repeat from * twice, join with sl st to 3rd ch at start.

Rnds 5 & 6: Repeat Rnd 4 twice — 21 dc on each side at end of Rnd 6.

Rnd 7: Ch 1, 1 sc in top of ch-3, work 1 sc in each dc around working 5 sc in each corner space, join with sl st to first sc. Fasten off.

Join Motifs: Motifs are crocheted together to form a rectangle 4 × 6 squares. First make 6 strips of 4 squares each, then join the 6 strips together. Join as follows: Place 2 squares with back sides together; crocheting through *both thicknesses* and working in *both loops* of each st, insert hook in center sc at corner, yo and draw up a loop, sl st in each st across ending in center sc at next corner; cut yarn and pull yarn end out through last st. Fasten off.

Border: A band of sc is made separately and then crocheted to outer edge of rug. The band is made a few inches longer as leeway in case of error when matching sts; excess sts are pulled out at end. Band — Right Side: Ch 550, work 1 sc in 2nd ch from hook and in each ch across, cut yarn and pull yarn out through last st to hold.

Join Band: With rug front side up, and band right side up with foundation chain to outer edge, crochet from rug side throught *both thicknesses* working in *both loops* of all sts. Starting at any corner of rug, insert hook in center sc of motif and first sc of band, yo and draw up a loop, * sl st in each st across motif ending in center sc at motif corner, sk seam, sl st in center sc at corner of next motif; repeat from * across to next corner of rug, sl st in each sc around corner; continue in this manner around to start. Pull out excess sts from band; fasten off, sewing ends of band together.

Fringe: (*Note: See p. 142 for instructions on knotting fringe.*) Wrap yarn around a 4" piece of cardboard. Cut yarn at one edge. Knot 1 strand in each loop of foundation chain of band on all sides. Trim evenly.

Blocking: Block with front side up; see p. 141 for blocking instructions.

Cleaning: Rug can be washed, but because of its size, dry cleaning is recommended. See p. 142 for dry cleaning information.

DETAIL OF FRONT MOTIF

DETAIL OF BACK MOTIF

Indian Rug

Color Photograph, p. 34

Inspiration can come from the least inspiring fonts of trivia — in this case, my "workbook." This is a haphazard collection of papers, pictures, notes, and various tidbits of creative possibilities that I have arranged in a series of looseleaf binders and through which I browse, upon occasion, in order to refresh my memory as to why it takes up a full shelf in my bookcase. It was during one of those infrequent perusals that I came across a design marked "Indian Motif." I liked the pattern and redesigned it for this rug — aptly titled from the source. I have no idea what Indian would claim it, but similar geometrics appeared in ancient Peruvian textile designs, so perhaps it's something the Incas conjured up.

The rug is worked with Reynolds Tapis Pingouin in the double crochet jacquard technique. If you've got more space on the walls than on the floor, use it as a wall hanging. Make two extra rows at the end, turn over and stitch to the back to make a tunnel, and hang on a rod like a tapestry.

SIZE: Approx. 42″ × 47″ plus 4″ fringe

MATERIALS:

Reynolds Tapis Pingouin Rug Yarn (1¾ oz. skeins):

4 skeins White #05
7 skeins Dk. Green #48
9 skeins Med. Green #02
16 skeins Red #43

Alternate: Any equivalent weight bulky rug yarn

Crochet Hook Size J
Tapestry Needle #13

GAUGE: 2 dc = 1 inch
2 rows = 1⅝ inches

NOTE: Before starting, refer to p. 145 for instructions on how to work jacquard crochet. Rug is worked with double crochet method. Each square on chart = 2 dc.

To Start — Row 1 (Right Side): With Red, ch 86, work 1 dc in 4th ch from hook and in each ch across — 84 dc counting beginning ch-3 as first dc.

Row 2: Turn, sl st in first dc, ch 2 — counts as first dc (*Note: For an even edge, always work turning ch in this manner*), work 1 dc in each dc across, end with 1 dc in top of end ch.

Follow chart for remainder of rug. Pattern starts with Row 3 on right side of work.

Fringe: (*Note: See p. 142 for instructions on knotting fringe.*) Wrap Red around a 5½″ piece of cardboard. Cut yarn at one edge. Knot one strand in each st at short ends.

Blocking: See blocking instructions on p. 141.

Cleaning: See cleaning instructions for Irish Crochet Rug on p. 17.

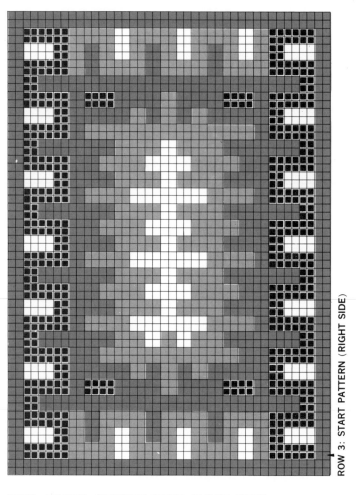

ROW 3: START PATTERN (RIGHT SIDE)

■ RED   □ WHITE   ■ MEDIUM GREEN   ■ DARK GREEN

3. Bedroom Accessories

Traditionally, a bedroom is a place in which to sleep but today the bed is almost incidental. For many, the bedroom has become a second living room, a quiet retreat for reading, relaxing, brunching, and weekend working, equipped with sofas, desks, and bookcases to accommodate the change-over.

Of course, size determines just how much living this new living room can offer, but whether you've got space for one bed or three sofas, the following pages provide a few ideas in crochet comfort that will fit in anywhere.

Patch-Quilt Bedspread

Color Photograph, p. 35

The revival of the quilt has brought back the patch — from patched jeans to patched beds. Back in the days when recycling was a way of life and thrift was the watchword of survival, everything was saved to be made over into something new. From fabric scraps and a little creative ingenuity the quilt was born, while odd pieces of yarn cleverly found their way into the granny afghan.

Here the two ideas are brought together as a crocheted patch-quilt bedspread. The motif is the same throughout, but the erratic color combinations create the patchwork look of a crazy quilt. Make it from scratch as shown, or if you're a scrap scrounger, this is a perfect project for yarn leftovers. It's worked with ten colors in a two-ply wool, but you can use as many colors as you like. If you'd rather use knitting worsted instead, the squares will come out larger; so fewer will be needed to make the same size spread.

Select colors at random as you work each round. Each motif has six color changes — the only color duplication within each motif is in the seventh round which repeats the color of the third round, limiting each motif to five colors. The squares are crocheted together with a white chain stitch border, then an edging is worked around the entire outer edge.

The directions and materials are given to fit a twin bed but you can make the spread larger by adding more squares. It's designed to reach just over the head end of the mattress; if you prefer to tuck in a pillow, add more rows of squares to the length.

SIZE: Approx. 60″ × 90″ (to fit twin bed)

MATERIALS:
Bucilla Wool and Shetland Wool (2 oz. skeins):
   3 skeins each of Fiesta Pink #278, Orange #294, Larkspur #230, and Emerald #297
   4 skeins each of Magnolia Pink #282, Scarlet #1009, Lime Twist #233, Sailing Blue #290, Pumpkin #332, and Lemon Pop #235
   9 skeins White #1
   Alternate: Any similar 2-ply wool, knitting worsted, or yarn scraps

GAUGE: Each motif is a 4¾″ square not including border

NOTE: All rnds are worked from right side. When starting a new rnd, attach new strand away from join or previous rnd. See p. 141 for helpful hint on working over joinings. Where possible, crochet over yarn ends as you work. Choose colors at random. There are a total of 187 motifs and no 2 should be exactly alike.

First Motif
Rnd 1 (Right Side): With First Color, ch 2, work 8 sc in 2nd ch from hook, join with sl st to first sc. *Do not break yarn.*

Rnd 2: Work first cluster as follows: ch 2, (yo and insert hook in same sc as join, yo and draw up a loop, yo and through 2 loops on hook) 3 times, yo and through all 4 loops on hook, * ch 3, work next cluster as follows: yo and insert hook in next sc, yo and draw up a loop, yo and through 2 loops on hook (yo and insert hook in same sc, yo and draw up a loop, yo and through 2 loops on hook) 3 times, yo and through all 5 loops on hook; repeat

MOTIF DETAIL

from * 6 times, ch 3, join with sl st to top of first cluster — 8 clusters. Fasten off.

Rnd 3: Attach Next Color in any space as follows: holding yarn at back of work, yo hook, then insert hook in space and under end of yarn, yo and draw up a loop, yo and through both loops on hook — sc made (*Note: Attach all new strands in this manner*), work 4 more sc in same space, * work 5 sc in next space; repeat from * around, join with sl st to first sc. Fasten off.

Rnd 4: Attach Next Color in center sc of any 5-sc group — sc made, work 2 more sc in same sc, 1 sc in next sc, (insert hook in next sc and draw up a loop) twice, yo and through all 3 loops on hook — dec made, 1 sc in next sc, * 3 sc in next sc, 1 sc in next sc, work dec over next 2 sc, 1 sc in next sc; repeat from * around, join with sl st to first sc. Fasten off.

Rnd 5: Attach Next Color in any dec — sc made, 1 sc in next sc, * work dec over next 2 sc, 1 hdc in next sc, 1 dc in next sc, work 1 tr, ch 3, 1 tr all in next dec — corner, 1 dc in next sc, 1 hdc in next sc, work dec over next 2 sc, 1 sc in each of next 3 sc; repeat from * 3 times ending last repeat with 2nd dec, 1 sc in next sc, join with sl st to first sc. Fasten off.

Rnd 6: Attach Next Color in any st — sc made, work 1 sc in each st around working 5 sc in each corner space, join with sl st to first sc. Fasten off.

Rnd 7: Attach Same Color as Rnd 3 in center sc at any corner — sc made, ch 1 (sc plus ch-1 count as first dc), 1 dc in same st — first cluster, ch 3, retaining last loop of each st on hook work 2 dc in same st, yo and through all 3 loops on hook — 2nd cluster of corner made, * (ch 1, sk next st, work cluster same as 2nd cluster in next st) 7 times, ch 1, sk next sc, work 1 cluster, ch 3, 1 cluster all in next sc — corner; repeat from * 3 times ending last repeat with 7 clusters, ch 1, join with sl st to top of first cluster. Fasten off.

Rnd 8: Attach White in any corner space — sc made, ch 5, 1 sc in same space, (ch 3, 1 sc in next ch-1 space) 8 times, * ch 3, work 1 sc, ch 5, 1 sc all in corner space, (ch 3, 1 sc in next ch-1 space) 8 times; repeat from * twice, ch 3, join with sl st to first sc. Fasten off.

Second Motif: Work same as First Motif through Rnd 7. Join Second Motif to First Motif in last rnd as follows: work Rnd 8 across first side same as First Motif, end with 1 sc in 2nd corner space, ch 2, remove hook, lay First Motif right side up; joining starts at lower left corner and continues across left side; from right side insert hook in center ch at lower left corner of First Motif, pick up dropped loop of Second Motif and draw loop through ch, ch 2, 1 sc in same corner space of Second Motif, * ch 1, remove hook, insert hook in center ch of next loop on First Motif, pick up dropped loop of Second Motif and draw loop through ch, ch 1, 1 sc in next ch-1 space of Second Motif; repeat from * across ending with 1 sc in corner space of Second Motif, ch 2, remove hook, insert hook in center ch at corner of First Motif, pick up dropped loop of Second Motif and draw loop through ch, ch 2, 1 sc in same corner space of Second Motif; complete Second Motif same as First Motif. When joining on 2 sides, continue around second side joining same as first side.

Assembly: Complete remaining motifs through Rnd 7 for a total of 187. Join motifs to form a rectangle with 17 rows of 11 motifs each. Work row by row, laying out one row at a time in a pleasing color arrangement.

Border
Rnd 1: From right side attach White in ch-5 space at any corner of bedspread — sc made, ch 1, 1 sc in same space, (ch 1, 1 sc in next loop) 10 times, * ch 1, sk joining, 1 sc in first loop of next motif just after joining, (ch 1, 1 sc in next loop) 9 times; repeat from * across to next corner of bedspread, ch 1, work 1 sc, ch 1, 1 sc all in ch-5 space; continue around outer edge in this manner, end with ch 1, join with sl st to first sc. *Do not break yarn.*
Rnd 2: Sl st in ch-1 space at corner, ch 1, work 1 sc, ch 1, 1 sc all in same space, * ch 1, 1 sc in next ch-1 space; repeat from * across to next corner, ch 1, work 1 sc, ch 1, 1 sc all in ch-1 space at corner; continue around in this manner ending with ch-1, join with sl st to first sc. *Do not break yarn.*
Rnd 3: Do not turn, work in reverse sc as follows: * *working toward right,* insert hook in next space, *hook over yarn* and draw up a loop, yo and through both loops on hook — sc made, ch 1; repeat from * around, join to first sc. Fasten off.

Blocking: See p. 141 for blocking instructions.

Cleaning: Have dry-cleaned. See p. 142 for dry cleaning information.

Irish Crochet Pillow Sham
Color Photograph, p. 35

The artistry of Irish crochet transforms an ordinary bed pillow into this lacy lattice of white roses. The pillow sham is made with wool yarn in traditional Irish rose motifs, which are crocheted together. Additional flowers are then worked over the stitches where the motif corners join. The back is made with the same motifs without the flowers, then joined to the front in a frilly picot ruffle. It fits over a queen-size bed pillow covered in a zippered case of contrasting color to set off the stitches. The sham is closed with buttons at one end for easy removal.

SIZE: Approx. 27½″ × 22″ plus 5″ ruffle

MATERIALS:
  Bucilla Wool and Shetland Wool (2 oz. skeins):
    11 skeins White
  Alternate: Any similar 2-ply wool

Crochet Hook Size G
11 Clear Flat Buttons — ½″ diam.
Queen-Size Bed Pillow (covered with a colored,
  zippered casing)

GAUGE: Each motif is 5½″ square

33

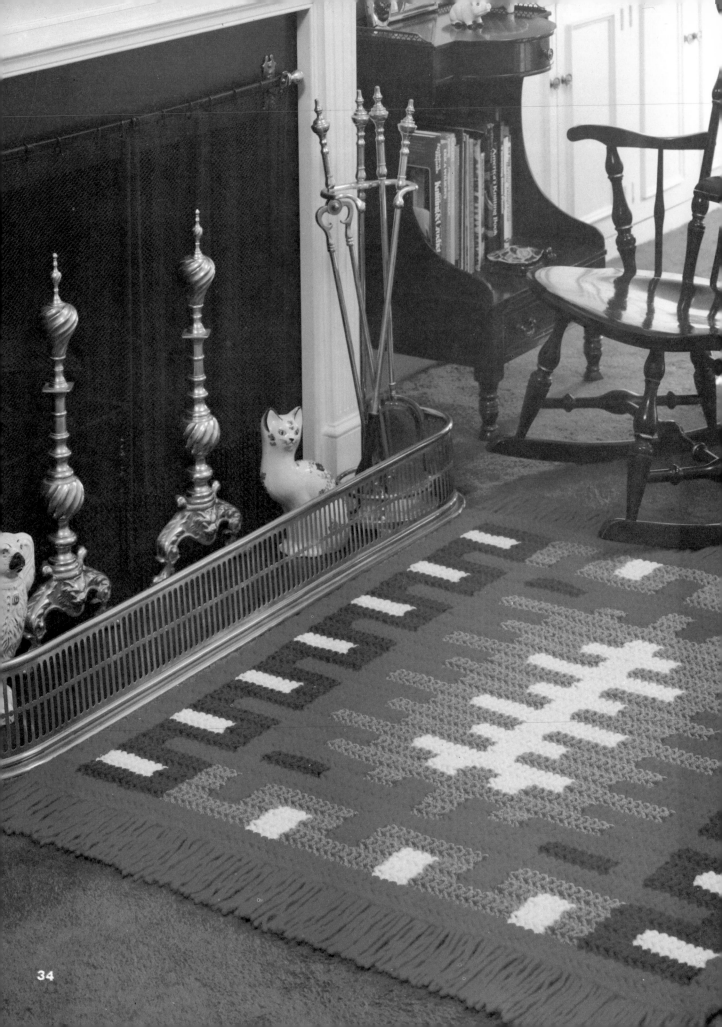

NOTE: All rnds are worked from right side. Work does not require blocking.

Front

First Motif — Rnd 1 (Right Side): Starting with flower, ch 7, work (1 dc, ch 3) 5 times all in 7th ch from hook, join with sl st to 3rd ch at start — 6 dc and 6 spaces.

Rnd 2: * In next space work: 1 sc, ch 1, (1 dc, ch 1) 4 times, and 1 sc — petal; repeat from * around, do not join — 6 petals.

Rnd 3: Ch 1, keeping petals forward insert hook under ch-3 of first rnd and work 1 sc around post, * ch 4, insert hook under next dc of first rnd and work 1 sc around post; repeat from * 4 times, ch 4, join with sl st to first sc — 6 loops.

Rnd 4: * Over next loop work: 1 sc, ch 1, (1 dc, ch 1) 5 times, and 1 sc — petal, ch 1; repeat from * around omitting ch-1 after last petal, join by working 1 sc in first sc — 6 petals.

Rnd 5: * Ch 4, keeping petals forward work 1 sc in ch-1 space between next 2 petals; repeat from * 4 times, ch 4, join with sl st to first sc — 6 loops.

Rnd 6: * Over next loop work: 1 sc, ch 1, (1 dc, ch 1) 8 times, and 1 sc — petal, ch 1; repeat from * around omitting ch-1 after last petal, join by working 1 sc in first sc — 6 petals.

Rnd 7: Ch 4, sl st in 3rd ch from hook — picot, ch 5, sl st in 3rd ch from hook — picot, ch 2 — double-picot-ch made, 1 sc in space between 4th and 5th dc of first petal, work double-picot-ch, 1 sc in ch-1 space between petals, * work double-picot-ch, 1 sc in space between 4th and 5th dc of next petal, work double-picot-ch, 1 sc in ch-1 space between petals; repeat from * around, join last double-picot-ch with sl st to first sc — 12 picot-loops.

Rnd 8: Keeping picot forward sl st in each of next 4 ch of first loop, 1 sc over same loop, ch 6, work picot, ch 3 — single-picot-ch made, 1 sc over next loop between picots, * work corner: ch 4, work picot, ch 9, sl st in 2nd ch from picot, ch 4, work picot, ch 2, 1 sc over next loop between picots, (work single-picot-ch, 1 sc over next loop between picots) twice; repeat from * around ending with single-picot-ch after last corner, join with sl st to first sc. Fasten off.

Second Motif: Work same as First Motif through Rnd 7. Join Second Motif to First Motif in last rnd as follows: sl st to center of first loop, 1 sc over same loop, ch 6, work picot, ch 3, 1 sc over next loop between picots; ch 4, work picot, ch 5, re-move hook, lay First Motif right side up; joining starts at lower left corner and continues across left side; from right side insert hook in 4th ch of corner loop of First Motif, pick up dropped ch of Second Motif and draw through st, ch 4, sl st in 2nd ch from picot of Second Motif, ch 4, work picot, ch 2, 1 sc over next loop of Second Motif between picots, * ch 4, remove hook, from right side insert hook in first ch after picot in next loop of First Motif, pick up dropped ch of Second Motif and draw through st, ch 4, 1 sc over next loop of Second Motif between picots; repeat from * once, ch 4, work picot, ch 5, remove hook, from right side insert hook in 4th ch of next corner loop of First Motif, pick up dropped ch of Second Motif and draw through st, ch 4, sl st in 2nd ch from picot, ch 4, work picot, ch 2, 1 sc over next loop of Second Motif between picots; complete Second Motif same as First Motif. When joining on 2 sides, continue around second side same as first side. Work a total of 20 motifs joined to form a rectangle with 4 rows of 5 motifs each.

Flowers: Flowers are worked on right side at each juncture where corner loops of 4 motifs are joined. Starting with any motif, attach yarn with sl st in center space formed by 4-corner join, working over right ch-section of any corner loop, work: 1 sc, (ch 1, 1 dc) 5 times; ch 3, work picot, working back toward center of join over left ch-section of same loop, work: (1 dc, ch 1) 5 times, and 1 sc — first petal made; starting with right ch-section of next motif, work second petal same as first petal. Continue in this manner until a petal is worked over all 4 corner loops, join with sl st to first sc of first petal. Fasten off. Work remainder of flowers same as first flower for total of 12 flowers.

Front Border: On right side of Front, attach yarn in any corner loop, work 5 sc over loop, * (ch 6, 1 sc over next loop to right of picot) twice, ch 6, 1 sc between corner loops of joining; repeat from * across ending with 5 sc over next corner loop: continue in this manner around remaining 3 sides, join with sl st to first sc. Fasten off.

Back

First Motif — Rnd 1 (Right Side): Ch 1 for center, ch 1 more, 1 sc in center ch, * ch 4, work picot, ch 5, work picot, ch 2 — double-picot-ch made, 1 sc in center ch; repeat from * 3 times, join last picot ch with sl st to first sc — 4 picot-loops.

Rnd 2: Keeping picot forward, sl st in each of next 4 ch of first loop, 1 sc over same loop, work

36

DETAIL OF FRONT MOTIFS

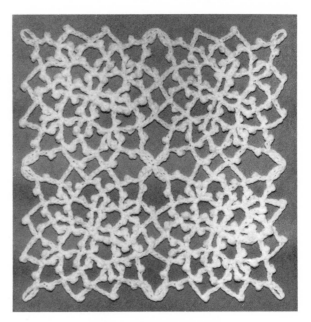

DETAIL OF BACK MOTIFS

double-picot-ch, 1 sc over same loop; * work double-picot-ch, 1 sc over next loop between picots, work double-picot-ch, 1 sc over same loop; repeat from * twice, work double-picot-ch, join with sl st to first sc — 8 picot-loops.

Rnd 3: Sl st to center of first loop, 1 sc over same loop, * work double-picot-ch, 1 sc in next loop between picots, work double-picot-ch, 1 sc in same loop, work double-picot-ch, 1 sc in next loop between picots; repeat from * 3 times, join last double-picot-ch with sl st to first sc — 12 picot-loops.

Rnd 4: Work same as Rnd 8 of Front Motif. Work remainder of motifs same as First Motif through Rnd 3, joining in last rnd same as Front Motif. Work a total of 20 motifs joined to form a rectangle with 4 rows of 5 motifs each.

Back Border: Working across short side of Back, from right side attach yarn in corner loop, work 5 sc over loop, * (ch 6, 1 sc in next loop to right of picot, ch 4, sl st in *side* of sc — buttonhole) twice, ch 6, 1 sc between corner loops of joining, work buttonhole; repeat from * across, end with 5 sc over next corner loop; continue around remaining 3 sides same as Front Border.

Ruffle: Front and Back are joined in first rnd of ruffle. Place wrong sides together; with Front side facing, hold pieces so that buttonhole end is toward the right.
First Corner: *Working through both thicknesses,*

attach yarn at lower right corner in first sc of 5-sc group, 1 sc in same sc, * ch 4, work picot, ch 5, work picot, ch 2 — double-picot-ch made, 1 sc in next sc; repeat from * 3 times.

Buttonhole Side: * Work double-picot-ch, 1 sc over next ch-6 loop of *front side only,* (work double-picot-ch, 1 sc over same loop) 3 times; repeat from * across side.

Second Corner: Work double-picot-ch, *working through both thicknesses* work 1 sc in first sc at corner, (work double-picot-ch, 1 sc in next sc) 4 times.

First Long Side: * Work double-picot-ch, *working through both thicknesses* work 1 sc over next ch-6 loop, (work double-picot-ch, 1 sc over same loop) 3 times; repeat from * across side.

Continue around remainder of cover, repeating Second Corner and First Long Side, end with double-picot-ch, join with sl st to first sc.

Next Rnd: Sl st to center of next loop, 1 sc in same loop, * work double-picot-ch, 1 sc in next loop between picots; repeat from * around ending with double-picot-ch, join with sl st to first sc. Repeat last rnd 5 times. Fasten off.

Finishing: Sew buttons on wrong side of Front, along edge at base of ruffle, to correspond to buttonholes. Place cover over pillow and button closed.

Cleaning: Either hand-wash according to washing instructions on p. 142 or have dry-cleaned. See p. 142 for dry cleaning information.

Lamp Shade

Color Photograph, p. 35

Here's an idea to add new life to an old lamp shade or fancy up a new one. Fashioned after the traditional boudoir table lamp, the crocheted cover gives it fresh flair. Although the directions are for a specific size shade (see dimensions under "Materials"), a variance of a half inch, plus or minus, won't make any difference. The cover has a fair amount of stretch and will conform to the shape of the shade. Use an untrimmed paper or fabric shade.

The cover is worked with cotton thread in a mesh of chain stitches with a ruffling of chains around the edges. To keep the cover from sliding, a strip of double-faced tape is pressed to the shade around the top and lower edges. It's referred to as mounting tape — the kind that has a thin foam padding between the adhesive surfaces. The "Scotch" brand comes in a continuous roll a half inch wide and you'll find it for sale with picture-hanging accessories. If you use a fabric shade, make sure the tape will stick.

MATERIALS:

Coats & Clark's Speed-Cro-Sheen Cotton:
  3 balls Hunter's Green
Alternate: Lily Double Quick Crochet Cotton
Crochet Hook Size 1
Lamp Shade — 5″ top diam., 8″ bottom diam.,
  6¾″ high
2 yds. Elastic Cord
Mounting Tape (½″ width) — in continuous
  length

NOTE: All rnds are worked from right side.

Rnd 1 (Right Side): Starting at top edge, ch 99 to fit around top rim of shade without stretching, taking care not to twist ch, join with sl st to first ch to make a ring, ch 1, 1 sc in same ch as join, * ch 4, sk next 2 ch, 1 sc in next ch; repeat from * around ending with ch-2 after last sc, join by working 1 dc in first sc — 33 loops.

Rnd 2: * Ch 4, 1 sc over center of next loop; repeat from * around ending with ch-2 after last sc, join by working 1 dc in joining-dc of last rnd. Repeat Rnd 2 for total of 20 rnds.

Next Rnd: Work same as Rnd 2 but end with ch-4, join with sl st in joining-dc of last rnd. *Do not break thread*

Bottom Ruffle — Row 1 (Elastic): Ch 1, holding elastic along edge of work with thread in front, and leaving a 4″ end, crochet over elastic as follows: insert hook under elastic in same dc as join, yo and draw up a loop, yo and through both loops on hook — sc made, * work 1 sc in *both loops* of each of next 4 ch, 1 sc in *back loop* of next sc; repeat from * around, join with sl st to both loops of first sc. Cut elastic leaving a 4″ end. *Do not break thread.*

Row 2: * Ch 4, sl st in *both loops* of next sc; repeat from * around, join with sl st to joining-sl st of last rnd. Fasten off.
Note: Turn work upside down and continue working from right side.

Row 3: Work on opposite side of elastic row in single loop of each st as follows: insert hook in any st and draw up a loop, ch 4, continue same as Row 2, join with sl st to first ch at start. Fasten off.

Top Ruffle

Note: In ch's where sc was previously worked, work in single loop of ch; work in both loops of ch's between sc's.

Row 1 (Elastic): Holding elastic along edge of work and leaving a 4″ end, crochet over elastic as follows: starting in any ch where sc is worked, yo hook, then insert hook in ch and under elastic and under end of thread, yo and draw up a loop, yo and through both loops on hook — sc made, work 1 sc in each ch around, join with sl st to both loops of first sc. Cut elastic leaving a 4″ end. *Do not break thread.*

Row 2: Work same as Row 2 of Bottom Ruffle.
Note: Turn work upside down and continue working from right side.

Row 3: Work on opposite side of elastic row in single loop of each st as follows: insert hook in *front loop* of foundation chain *under* any sc of Rnd 1 (hold sc to left side to insert hook), draw up a loop, (ch 4, sl st in next ch) twice, ch 4, sl st in *front loop* of next ch *under* sc; continue around in this manner, join with sl st to first ch at start. Fasten off.

Tie Elastic: At top and bottom, draw up each end of elastic about 3″ and knot securely. Weave ends of elastic back through sts on wrong side.

Assembly

1. Measure perimeter of shade at lower edge.
2. Cut mounting tape in half *lengthwise* to make two ¼″ strips cut to these measurements.
3. Press tape to outside edge of rim at top and bottom.
4. Stretch cover over shade and press base of ruffle to tape.

Cleaning: Pull cover from tape and remove. Wash according to washing instructions on p. 142. Lay flat to dry. Let dry thoroughly and replace on shade. Tape may have to be replaced.

Striped Afghan and Matching Pillow

Color Photograph, p. 43

Since afghan designs abound in multitudinous proportions, only two are included. Both are made with four-ply knitting worsted.

This one is worked in a diagonal basket weave pattern based on double crochet and slip stitches. Work begins at one corner, expands to a rectangular shape and ends at the diagonally opposite corner. The combined effect of the tricolor stripes (see color photograph) and the random coloring of the variegated yarn creates a striking design.

It's framed in a chain stitch border which is carried through in the ruffle around a matching pillow worked from the same instructions. The pillow cover is closed with buttons at one end for easy removal.

Variations: Try another version — rainbow stripes. Use one color to a row and repeat the following color sequence: Red, Medium Orange, Light Orange, Lime Green, Purple, and Lavender. This is also an ideal project for yarn leftovers. Make each row a different color, or alternate each color row with black if extra yarn is needed.

Directions are given for the afghan. Use same directions for pillow following changes in parentheses. For pillow make two sections the same.

AFGHAN SIZE: Approx. 45″ × 65″ plus 1″ border

PILLOW SIZE: Approx. 16½″ × 9½″ plus 2″ ruffle

MATERIALS:
   Bear Brand De Luxe Ombree Knitting Worsted (3½ oz. Twin-Paks):
      Afghan:
         5 Twin-Paks each of Blue #02 and Green #04
         7 Twin-Paks Rose #07
      Pillow:
         1 Twin-Pak each of Blue and Green
         2 Twin-Paks Rose
   Crochet Hook Size G
   6 Clear Flat Buttons (for pillow) — ½″ diam.
   Pillow Form — see p. 44

GAUGE: Measuring diagonally, 3 clusters = 2½ inches
            Measuring across rows, 4 clusters = 2½ inches
            (Work tightly for best results.)

NOTE: Each stripe consists of 3 rows. Stripes repeat in the following color sequence: Rose, Blue, Green. Make tags for markers with notes to identify corners and sides. Use safety pins to attach. Markers are used only as a shaping guide. A note on variegated yarn: When adding a new strand of the same color, match shade of new strand with same shade where previous yarn leaves off so that correct shading is maintained.

Row 1 (Right Side): Starting at corner, with Rose, ch 6, 1 dc in 4th ch from hook and in each of next 2 ch — cluster made. *Mark cluster as Bottom Corner.*
Row 2: Ch 6, turn, on wrong side of ch work 1 dc in 4th ch from hook and in each of next 2 ch, from wrong side sl st in space between last dc and ch-3 of first cluster made, ch 3, 3 dc in same space working sts over length of ch — 2 clusters. *Mark last dc of last cluster as Bottom End.*
Row 3: Ch 6, turn, 1 dc in 4th ch from hook and in each of next 2 ch, * sl st in ch-3 space of next cluster, ch 3, 3 dc in same space; repeat from * once, work off last 2 loops of last dc with Next Color — 3 clusters. *Mark last dc of last cluster as First Side.*
Row 4: Ch 6, turn, 1 dc in 4th ch from hook and in each of next 2 ch, * sl st in ch-3 space of next cluster, ch 3, 3 dc in same space; repeat from * across.
Repeat Row 4 for pattern. At end of each 3-row stripe, work off last 2 loops of last dc with Next Color. Work in pattern for total of 23 (5) stripes ending with Blue stripe (right side), work off last 2 loops of last dc with Next Color — 69 (15) clusters. *Mark beginning cluster of last Blue row as Bottom Corner.*

Note: Last cluster on Row 1 of next stripe starts second side.
Next Stripe — Row 1: Repeat Row 4, end with sl st in ch-3 space of last cluster.
Row 2: Ch 1, turn, sl st in each of next 3 dc and in ch-3 space of first cluster, ch 3, 3 dc in same space, * sl st in ch-3 space of next cluster, ch 3, 3 dc in same space; repeat from * across.
Row 3: Repeat Row 4 ending with sl st in ch-3 space of last cluster. Fasten off.

Next Stripe — Row 1: Turn, attach Next Color in ch-3 space of first cluster, ch 3, 3 dc in same space, * sl st in ch-3 space of next cluster, ch 3, 3 dc in same space; repeat from * across.
Row 2: Repeat Row 4 ending with sl st in ch-3 space of last cluster.
Row 3: Ch 1, turn, sl st in each of next 3 dc and in ch-3 space of first cluster, ch 3, 3 dc in same space, * sl st in ch-3 space of next cluster, ch 3, 3 dc in same space; repeat from * across, work off last 2 loops of last dc with Next Color.
Repeat last 2 stripes for total of 33 (9) stripes ending with Green stripe (right side) — 69 (15) clusters. Fasten off. *Mark last cluster of last row as Top Corner.*

Note: First cluster on Row 1 of next stripe starts top end.
Next Stripe — Row 1: Turn, attach Next Color in ch-3 space of first cluster, * ch 3, 3 dc in same

STITCH DETAIL

space, sl st in ch-3 space of next cluster; repeat from * across.

Row 2: Ch 1, turn, sl st in each of next 3 dc and in ch-3 space of first cluster, * ch 3, 3 dc in same space, sl st in ch-3 space of next cluster; repeat from * across.

Row 3: Repeat last row. Fasten off.

Repeat last stripe for total of 55 (13) stripes ending with Rose stripe (right side) — 3 clusters.

Last Stripe — Row 1: Turn, attach Blue in ch-3 space of first cluster, * ch 3, 3 dc in same space, sl st in ch-3 space of next cluster; repeat from * once — 2 clusters.

Row 2: Ch 1 — turn, sl st in each of next 3 dc and in ch-3 space of first cluster, ch 3, 3 dc in same space, sl st in ch-3 space of next cluster — 1 cluster. Fasten off. Remove markers.

Afghan Border

Note: All rnds are worked from right side. Each rnd is started with a new strand to avoid making seam.

Rnd 1: From right side attach Rose in any corner, work 1 sc, ch 2, 1 sc all in same corner, ** * ch 2, 1 sc between next 2 clusters; repeat from * across side ending with 1 sc between last 2 clusters, ch 2, work 1 sc, ch 2, 1 sc all in next corner; repeat from ** around, end with 1 sc between last 2 clusters before corner of start, ch 2, join with sl st to first sc. Fasten off.

Rnd 2: Starting at another corner, attach Rose in corner space, 1 sc in same space, ** * ch 2, 1 sc in next sc; repeat from * across ending with 1 sc in last sc before corner space, ch 2, 1 sc in corner space; repeat from ** around ending with 1 sc in last sc before starting corner, ch 2, join with sl st to first sc. Fasten off.

Rnd 3: Starting at another corner, attach Rose in corner-sc, work 1 sc, ch 2, 1 sc all in same sc, ** * ch 2, 1 sc in next sc; repeat from * across ending with 1 sc in last sc before corner-sc, ch 2, work 1 sc, ch 2, 1 sc all in corner-sc; repeat from ** around ending with 1 sc in last sc before corner of start, ch 2, join with sl st to first sc. Fasten off. Repeat Rnds 2 & 3 once.

Pillow Border: Work border around each pillow section same as Rnd 1 of Afghan Border. Join the 2 pieces as follows: hold pieces together with wrong sides facing; crocheting through *both thicknesses* and working across short end, attach Rose in corner space, 1 sc in same space, * ch 2, 1 sc in next sc, ch 2, 1 sc in next ch-2 space * ; repeat from * to * once, ch 2, 1 sc in next sc. For opening, work through *front side only* as follows: ch 2, 1 sc in next ch-2 space; repeat from * to * 10 times; *working through both thicknesses* again, repeat from * to * around ending with 1 sc in last sc before corner of start, ch 2, join with sl st to first sc. Fasten off.

Ruffle: Repeat Rnds 3 & 2 of Afghan Border for 7 more rows.

Pillow Form: Cut 2 pieces of muslin 11½" × 18½" and follow instructions for making pillow form on p. 143.

Finishing: At open end, on wrong side sew buttons at base of ruffle opposite every other ch-2 loop. Use chain-loops as buttonholes. Insert pillow form and button closed.

Blocking: Block afghan according to blocking instructions on p. 141. Pillow does not require blocking.

Cleaning: Afghan and pillow cover may be hand-washed according to washing instructions on p. 142, but because of its size, dry cleaning is recommended for the afghan. See dry cleaning information on p. 142.

Square Afghan

Color Photograph, p. 42

The design for this rather unconventional afghan was adapted from an embroidery pattern, crocheted into colorful flower motifs — all sewn together in a square of squares. It's finished off with a braided border around the edges and fringed on all sides. Fold it over the back of a sofa to keep handy as a lap throw, or use it as a crib cover to warm up a toddler with a little handmade love.

SIZE: Approx. 43″ × 43″ plus 3″ fringe

MATERIALS:
4-ply Knitting Worsted:
24 oz. Royal Blue (Main Color — MC)
4 oz. each of Lt. Blue, Lt. Pink, Dk. Pink, Yellow, Avocado Green, and White
2 oz. each of Orange, Lt. Aqua, and Dk. Aqua
Crochet Hook Size G
Crochet Hook Size J (used for braid only)
Tapestry Needle #17

GAUGE: Small Motif is a 2⅝″ square
Large Motif is a 5⅝″ square

NOTE: All rnds are worked from right side. Identifying numbers refer to motif arrangement in diagram.

First Small Motif (Contrasting Center)
   Make: 16 Dk. Aqua with Yellow Center (#1)
   16 Orange with Yellow Center (#2)
   16 Lt. Aqua with Yellow Center (#3)
   16 Lt. Blue with Yellow Center (#4)
   16 Yellow with Orange Center (#5)
Rnd 1 (Right Side): With Center Color and G Hook, ch 2, work 8 sc in 2nd ch from hook, join with sl st to first sc. Fasten off.
Rnd 2: Attach Next Color in any sc as follows: holding yarn at back of work, yo hook, then from right side insert hook in st and under end of yarn, yo and draw up a loop, yo and through both loops on hook — sc made (*Note: Attach all new strands in this manner*), ch 4 (sc plus ch-4 count as first tr and ch-1 space), 1 tr in same sc, ch 1, work 1 tr, ch 1, 1 tr all in next sc, ch 3 — corner, * (work 1 tr, ch 1, 1 tr all in next sc, ch 1) twice, ch 2 more for corner; repeat from * twice, ch 2 more, join with sl st to 3rd ch at start. Fasten off.
Rnd 3: Attach MC in any corner space — sc made, ch 3, 1 sc in same space, (ch 1, 1 sc in next ch-1 space) 3 times, * ch 1, work 1 sc, ch 3, 1 sc all in corner space, (ch 1, 1 sc in next ch-1 space) 3 times; repeat from * twice, ch 1, join with sl st to first sc. Fasten off.

Second Small Motif (Non-Contrasting Center)
   Make: 16 Lt. Blue (#6)
   32 Green (#7)
   32 Lt. Pink (#8)
   32 Dk. Pink (#9)
Rnd 1: Work same as Rnd 1 of First Small Motif. *Do not break yarn.*

Rnd 2: Ch 5, 1 tr in same sc as join, continue same as Rnd 2 of First Small Motif, join with sl st to 4th ch at start. Fasten off.
Rnd 3: Work same as Rnd 3 of First Small Motif.

Large Motif
   Make: 16 the same (#10)
Rnds 1 & 2: With Yellow work same as Rnds 1 & 2 of Second Small Motif.
Rnd 3: Attach White in any corner space — sc made, ch 3 (sc plus ch-3 count as first dc and ch-1 space), work 1 dc, ch 3, 1 dc, ch 1, 1 dc all in same space, (ch 1, 1 dc in next ch-1 space) 3 times, * ch 1, work 1 dc, ch 1, 1 dc, ch 3, 1 dc, ch 1, 1 dc all in corner space, (ch 1, 1 dc in next ch-1 space) 3 times; repeat from * twice, ch 1, join with sl st to 2nd ch at start.
Rnd 4: Ch 4, 1 dc in next dc, ch 1, work 1 dc, ch 3, 1 dc all in corner space, * (ch 1, 1 dc in next dc) 7 times, ch 1, work 1 dc, ch 3, 1 dc all in corner space; repeat from * twice, (ch 1, 1 dc in next dc) 5 times, ch 1, join with sl st to 3rd ch at start.
Rnd 5: Ch 4, (1 dc in next dc, ch 1) twice, work 1 dc, ch 3, 1 dc all in corner space, * (ch 1, 1 dc in next dc) 9 times, ch 1, work 1 dc, ch 3, 1 dc all in corner space; repeat from * twice, (ch 1, 1 dc in next dc) 6 times, ch 1, join with sl st to 3rd ch at start. Fasten off.
Rnd 6: Attach MC in any corner space — sc made, ch 3, 1 sc in same space, (ch 1, 1 sc in next ch-1 space) 10 times, * ch 1, work 1 sc, ch 3, 1 sc all in corner space, (ch 1, 1 sc in next ch-1 space) 10 times; repeat from * twice, ch 1, join with sl st to first sc. Fasten off.

Assembly
Sew motifs together according to Arrangement Diagram. Refer to motif identifying number for color placement.
Sewing Sequence: Join Small Motifs to form strips as shown, then sew the strips to Large Motif in letter sequence to form one large square.

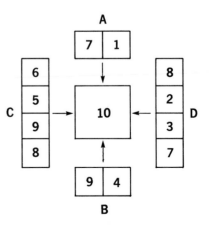

Combine motifs in this manner to make 16 large squares. Sew the large squares together in 4 rows of 4 squares so that motifs are in the same position throughout. To make sewing come out even when joining strips to Large Motif, on each strip count seam as 1 st and count center ch of each motif corner at each side of seam as 1 st.

Sewing: Using MC and tapestry needle, sew from right side with overcast stitch (*Note: See diagram on p. 143*). Insert needle through *both loops* of each sc and each ch st. Start sewing in center ch at one corner and end in center ch at next corner. Work with an even tension to keep seam as elastic as motifs.

Finishing

Border: Attach MC in ch-3 space at one corner of afghan — sc made, ch 3 (sc plus ch-3 count as first dc and ch-1 space), work (1 dc, ch 1) twice and 1 dc all in same space, * (ch 1, 1 dc in next ch-1 space) 4 times, ch 1, 1 dc in next space just before seam, ch 1, sk seam, 1 dc in first space of next motif directly after seam; repeat from * across to next afghan corner ending in ch-1 space just before corner space, ch 1, work (1 dc, ch 1) 3 times and 1 dc all in corner space, continue around in this manner ending with ch-1, join with sl st to 2nd ch at start. Fasten off.

Braid: The braid is formed by slip stitching over the double crochet stitches of the border. Work with 3 strands of MC held together as 1 strand. Use an even tension to keep braid as elastic as rest of work. Holding yarn at back of work, from right side insert J Hook in any space, yo at back and draw up a loop through space, * working toward left, insert hook in next space, yo hook at back, draw up a loop through space and then through loop on hook — sl st made; repeat from * around ending in space just before starting space. To finish off ends, cut yarn leaving strands 10″ long, pull ends out through last sl st to front, insert hook *under* the top 2 loops of *first* sl st made and pull yarn ends through loops out to one side; from wrong side insert hook *between* the top 2 loops of *last* sl st made and draw yarn to wrong side. Fasten off by weaving beginning and end strands through dc's on wrong side.

Fringe: (*Note: See p. 142 for instructions on knotting fringe.*) Wrap MC around a piece of cardboard 4″ wide, cut yarn at one side; combine 3 strands for one fringe, knot a fringe in each space next to braid around entire afghan, trim evenly.

Blocking: See blocking instructions on p. 141.

Cleaning: Afghan can be hand-washed, but because of its size, dry cleaning is recommended. See p. 142 for dry cleaning information.

4. Furniture Applications

Among the needle arts, needlepoint has long been the standard for upholstery fabrics, particularly because of its durability and exceptional patterns. But crochet too, when properly planned, provides a reliable source for upholstery materials with surprisingly successful results.

Upholstery is continually plagued by environmental attacks from body friction and oils, dirt, dust, and humidity changes — all serious challengers to the life of furniture coverings. To help resist the persistence of wear and tear, only certain yarn fibers are practical — either needlepoint yarn (Persian or tapestry wool) or tightly twisted cotton thread. Both will hold up for a long period of time. The fabric must be crocheted as tightly as possible in a solid pattern of stitches to produce a tough, durable piece of material that won't overly stretch or be an easy target for thread pulls.

Needlepoint yarn is available in skeins with enough yardage for a workable span of continuous crocheting. Although it's expensive, the color range almost makes up for the cost, but the main advantage is its rich visual and textural qualities. All of the samples crocheted in cotton are made with Coats & Clark's Speed-Cro-Sheen with specific color names listed, but Lily Double Quick crochet cotton will work just as well, though not all colors are the same.

The fabric doesn't have to be crocheted to fit the item it will cover. It's simply cut to shape and treated the same as a regular piece of cloth fabric with stitching worked around the raw edge to prevent raveling.

The furniture treatments shown are by no means limited to the sample items. They're just stimulators to get you started on your own projects. Five fabric patterns are given, any of which can be made with cotton thread or needlepoint yarn. Select a fabric, choose your own colors, and turn it into whatever you like.

Director's Chair

Color Photograph, p. 55

Where once sat the kings of Hollywood to elevate their status, now sit us common folk tuning in the Late Show to watch what all that status got us. The director's chair has come a long way from the back lot movie set and today almost no household is home without one.

They come in everything from bamboo to gold plate and run rampant with what stretches across them. Add another idea — crocheted bargello. The fabric is worked with cotton thread in a single crochet ripple pattern mounted on canvas for support. The back is tubular so the design appears on both sides.

Instructions are for a specific size chrome frame (see ''Mounting Materials'' for dimensions). Unfortunately these chairs are not manufactured to a standard size, so you'll have to do a little measuring. If your chair frame varies no more than a half inch, plus or minus, from the listed measurements, follow the directions as given. If there is a larger variance, you will probably have to alter the size of the crocheted fabric. To change the length of the seat, increase or decrease one or more ripples. To change the length of the back, increase or decrease by multiples of two ripples to maintain the correct number of points for proper alignment. To alter the width of the seat or back, increase or decrease one or more stripes, or half a stripe at beginning and end. If you do change the dimensions of the fabric, remember to make corresponding changes in the mounting instructions.

When buying a new chair, try to get the size specified. If you have difficulty finding the correct size or any chair of this type, Bon Marché in New York City carries them and gladly accepts mail orders. Each chair costs about $30 and comes with a vinyl seat and back. Address your inquiries to: Bon Marché, 74 Fifth Avenue, New York, N.Y. 10011.

A note on removing the seat rods: My initial bout with this mechanical maneuver was like confronting a fiendish Chinese puzzle. I don't know what ingenious device you might find on yours, but mine has a small pin at each end of the seat rods. With a hammer and a round-ended screwdriver (Phillips head) knock one pin from each rod and the rods will pull out.

A note on hinged wood frames: These chairs are generally larger than the chrome ones (for bigger directors?) and all of the dimensions will have to be altered if you prefer to use this type of frame. For mounting, use the canvas supports specifically made for these chairs. The length and width of the back and the width of the seat will have to be increased. The length of the seat must be decreased so the crocheted fabric ends flush with the base of the arm rest. The seat will not fit if fabric extends under the base. Follow instructions only as a guide and use your own judgment when making alterations.

SIZE: See chair frame dimensions on p. 51.

CROCHET MATERIALS:
Coats & Clark's Speed-Cro-Sheen Cotton:
4 balls each of Hunter's Green, Blue Sparkle, Canary Yellow, and Spanish Red
Crochet Hook Size 1

GAUGE: 1 ripple from point to point = 1⅛ inches
4 rows = ¾ inch
(Work tightly — gauge must be maintained.)

NOTE: Stripes repeat in the following color sequence: Green, Blue, Green, Blue, Yellow, Red, Yellow, Red.

Seat
Row 1 (Right Side): With First Color, ch 183, 1 sc in 2nd ch from hook and in each of next 4 ch, * 3 sc in next ch — top point, 1 sc in each of next 3 ch, sk next 2 ch — bottom point, 1 sc in each of next 3 ch; repeat from * across ending in 7th ch from end, 3 sc in next ch, 1 sc in each of next 5 ch — 20 top points. Fasten off.
Row 2: Turn, attach Next Color as follows: holding thread at back of work, yo hook, then insert hook in first st and under end of thread, yo and draw up a loop, insert hook in next st and draw up a loop, yo and through all 3 loops on hook — dec made, 1 sc in each of next 4 sts, * 3 sc in next st — top point, 1 sc in each of next 3 sts, sk next 2 sts — bottom point, 1 sc in each of next 3 sts; repeat from * across ending with 3 sc in last top point, 1 sc in each of next 4 sts, dec as follows: (insert hook in next st and draw up a loop) twice, yo and through all 3 loops on hook. Fasten off.
Repeat Row 2 for total of 68 rows — 17 broad stripes.

Border: Working on foundation chain edge with Matching Color, from right side sl st in each single loop of ch across. Fasten off. Working along last row with Matching Color, from right side sl st in each sc across. Fasten off.

Blocking: Block Seat according to blocking instructions on p. 141 to 13″ wide at sides and 24″ long.

Back
Note: Each rnd is started at a new place to avoid making seam.
Rnd 1 (Right Side): With First Color, ch 306, *taking care not to twist ch,* join with sl st to first ch to form a ring, ch 1, 1 sc in same ch, 3 sc in next ch — top point, 1 sc in each of next 3 ch, * sk next 2 ch — bottom point, 1 sc in each of next 3 ch, 3 sc in next ch — top point, 1 sc in each of next 3 ch;

repeat from * around ending in 5th ch from start, sk next 2 ch, 1 sc in each of next 2 ch, join with sl st to first sc — 34 top points. Fasten off.

Rnd 2: Turn, attach Next Color in center sc of any top point away from previous joining, 3 sc in same st, * 1 sc in each of next 3 sts, sk next 2 sts — bottom point, 1 sc in each of next 3 sts, 3 sc in next st — top point; repeat from * around ending with 3 sc after last bottom point, join with sl st to first sc. Fasten off.

Repeat Row 2 for total of 36 rows — 9 broad stripes. (*Last row is top edge.*)

Blocking: With right side out, lay Back flat on pressing board so that ends crease at center of points on top edge. Pin to 7″ wide at sides and 20″ long. Block same as Seat.

MOUNTING MATERIALS:

Chrome Chair Frame
    Seat: 19½″ long (measuring from outside edge of rods)
        13⅝″ wide (length of rods *between* frame)
    Back: 19½″ long (measuring from outside edge of bars)
        8¼″ wide (length of bars from arm rests)
1¼ yds. Medium Weight Dark Blue Canvas — washed and ironed
2 yds. Fusible Web (Stitch Witchery or Magic Polyweb)

STITCH DETAIL

Clear (Invisible) Nylon Sewing Thread
Sewing Machine

Assembly

Note: Wash and iron canvas before starting. Thread sewing machine with clear nylon thread. Tension may have to be adjusted slightly – test on a scrap of fabric first. Work with 10 stitches to 1 inch unless otherwise specified.

Seat

1. Cut a rectanglar piece of canvas 14½″ × 26″.

2. Turn under each long edge 1″ to one side (which becomes wrong side) and press. Sewing through both thicknesses, make 3 rows of stitching ¼″ apart over each turn-under.

3. Turn under each short edge 1″ to wrong side. Press and stitch same as long edges. Canvas measures 12½″ × 24″.

4. Cut fusible web slightly larger than finished canvas. Lay web on wrong side of canvas and hand baste around all edges. Trim excess web.

5. Place canvas and crocheted fabric together with wrong sides facing. (Crocheted fabric may have to be stretched slightly to fit canvas.) Pin pieces together so that crocheted points extend ½″ beyond canvas on long sides; match edges evenly on short sides. Hand-baste around all edges.

6. From canvas side, machine-stitch ⅛″ in from edge on all sides. Make another row of stitching ⅛″ in from first row. Remove basting threads.

7. With canvas side up, pin seat to pressing board, stretching fabric evenly until canvas is smooth. Following fusible web directions, fuse the two pieces together pressing iron on *canvas side only.*

8. When dry (approx. 10 min.), turn under short ends about 3″ to canvas side, *matching points.* (Width of turn-under may vary depending on chair dimensions. Pin turn-under first and check fit. Seat should be stretched as tightly as possible.)

9. Set machine for 8 stitches to 1 inch and adjust presser foot for heavy fabric. From canvas side, stitch ⅛″ in from edge of each turn-under through all thicknesses. Make 2 more rows of stitching ¼″ apart over each turn-under.

10. Insert rods through tunnels at each side. Attach rods to chair so that first row of crochet is at front.

Back

Note: Reset machine for 10 stitches to 1 inch and reset presser foot for normal fabric.

1. Cut a rectangular piece of canvas 8″ × 42″.

2. Place short ends together and sew 1″ from

edge. Stitch again over first row to reinforce. Press seam open. Sewing through both thicknesses, stitch over each seam allowance ½" from seam.

3. Turn under each long edge 1" to wrong side and press. Sewing through both thicknesses, make 3 rows of stitching ¼" apart over each turn-under. Canvas measures 6" × 40".

4. Cut fusible web slightly larger than finished canvas. Lay web on wrong side of canvas, overlapping short ends ½". Hand-baste to canvas around edges. Trim excess web.

5. Place canvas and crocheted fabric together with wrong sides facing and with crocheted fabric on *outside* of tube. (Crocheted fabric may have to be stretched slightly to fit canvas.) Pin pieces together so that crocheted points extend ½" beyond edge of canvas. Hand-baste around edges.

6. From canvas side (inside tube), machine-stitch ⅛" in from each edge of canvas. Make another row of stitching ⅛" in from first row. Remove basting threads.

7. Working in sections, pin (with canvas side up) about 10" of tube at a time to pressing board, stretching fabric evenly until canvas is smooth. Fuse the two pieces together pressing iron on *canvas side only*.

8. When dry, lay Back flat with canvas sides together, so that ends crease at center of points on top edge. Mark center sc on each of these points.

9. Crochet top edges together: Working from crocheted side and counting either marked sc as first st, continue counting *backward* and insert hook in 14th sc from marked st (bottom point), yo with Matching Color and draw up a loop; working forward, sl st in each of next 26 sc; crease ends again at markers to align points, working through *both thicknesses,* sl st in each sc across next 14 ripples (ripple is counted from bottom point to bottom point); working through *single thickness only,* sl st in each remaining 27 sc. Fasten off.

10. Crochet bottom edges together (*Note: Work in single loop of foundation ch*): Align points on bottom edges to correspond to top. With Matching Color, starting at point directly opposite start of either top opening, and working through *single thickness,* sl st around to match top opening; working through *both thicknesses,* sl st in each ch across points ending at point directly opposite start of next top opening; working through *single thickness,* sl st around remaining sts to match top opening. Fasten off.

11. Set machine for 8 stitches to 1 inch and adjust presser foot for heavy fabric. Sewing through all thicknesses, stitch across each short end along a line the same width as openings. (Stretch a piece of masking tape across ends as a guide for straight line.) Make another row of stitching ⅛" toward center from first row.

12. Slide Back over supporting bars of chair with bottom edge down.

Cleaning: Have dry-cleaned. See dry cleaning information on p. 142.

Circular Chair Seat

Color Photograph, p. 54

At the turn of the century, young ladies were demurely sipping sodas with their young beaux against the white tile and stained-glass ambiance of the local ice-cream parlor — all under the watchful eye of the suspendered and pin-striped proprietor. Down the street the neighborhood barber pole was spinning in the trade for haircuts, while the shop quartet lamented over "That Old Gang of Mine" between shaves. Around the corner the organ grinder was sharing his hat with passersby, amusing his sidewalk clientele with gay airs and a dancing monkey. That's where the ice-cream parlor chair fit in seventy-five years ago; now it fits into my kitchen, quite undaunted by its epochal past life.

When it entered my home it was sadly without seat or love. I wanted to do something other than the original plain wood disc and hit upon the idea of an archery target. The brightly colored concentric rings adapted perfectly to a round seat; not exactly what they had in mind back in the nineties, but with the same gay spirit.

The cover is worked in rounds of single crochet and placed over a padded Masonite or plywood circle. If you don't happen to have an ice-cream parlor chair, the cover will work equally well as an upholstery piece for any round-seated chair or stool, or as a seat cushion. The directions will accommodate any size.

SIZE SHOWN: 15″ Diam. Seat

CROCHET MATERIALS (for size shown):
Coats & Clark's Speed-Cro-Sheen Cotton:
1 ball each of Canary Yellow, Spanish Red, Parakeet Blue, and Black
3 balls White
Crochet Hook Size 1
Tapestry Needle #17

GAUGE: 6 sc = 1 inch
6 rows = 1 inch

NOTE: All rnds are worked from right side. Each rnd is started at a new place to avoid making seam. See p. 141 for helpful hint on crocheting over joinings. Crochet over thread ends as you work. For seat as shown, work color sequence as follows: 9 rnds each of Yellow, Red, Blue, Black, and White; 1 rnd Black, 7 rnds White.

Rnd 1 (Right Side): With Yellow, ch 2, work 6 sc in 2nd ch from hook, join with sl st to first sc. Fasten off.

Rnd 2: Attach Yellow in any st as follows: holding thread at back of work, yo hook, then insert hook in st and under end of thread, yo and draw up a loop, yo and through both loops on hook — sc made (*Note: Attach all new strands in this manner*), 1 sc in same st, work 2 sc in each st around, join with sl st to first sc — 12 sc. Fasten off.

Rnd 3: Attach Yellow in any st — sc made, 1 sc in same st — inc, 1 sc in next st, * 2 sc in next st — inc, 1 sc in next st; repeat from * around, join with sl st to first sc — 18 sc. Fasten off.

Rnd 4: Attach Yellow in any *single* sc — sc made, 1 sc in same st, 1 sc in each of next 2 sts, * 2 sc in next st, 1 sc in each of next 2 sts; repeat from * around, join with sl st to first sc — 24 sc. Fasten off.

Rnd 5: Attach Yellow in any st other than inc — sc made, 1 sc in same st, 1 sc in each of next 3 sts, * 2 sc in next st, 1 sc in each of next 3 sts; repeat from * around, join with sl st to first sc — 30 sc. Fasten off.
Continue in this manner, increasing 6 sts on each

rnd. Space increases evenly and be careful not to increase directly over increase of last rnd. Cover can be made larger or smaller by increasing or decreasing the number of rnds of each color. Always work the same number of rnds of each color to keep the width of the circles consistent.

Slip Stitching
Note: A row of slip stitching is worked around the last rnd of each circle of finished cover. Place a marker anywhere along edge of cover. So that stitching all goes in the same direction, always start each rnd of slip stitching from same side of circle as marker. Work with an even tension. Avoid working too tightly.
Work Yellow Circle as follows: Holding thread at back of work, from right side insert hook *in between* any 2 sc of last Yellow rnd, yo at back and draw up a loop, * working toward left, insert hook *in between* next 2 sc, yo hook at back, draw up a loop and then through loop on hook — sl st made; repeat from * around ending between last 2 sc before start. To finish off end: Cut thread leaving a 7″ strand, pull thread out through last st to front; insert hook *under* the top 2 loops of *first* sl st made and pull thread through loops out to one side; from wrong side insert hook *between* the top 2 loops of *last* sl st made and draw thread to wrong side. Fasten off.
Work slip stitching the same over last rnd of each remaining circle including black stripe at edge.

Drawstring: Thread a 5′ strand (or longer if circle is larger) on tapestry needle. Weave needle in and out through each sc on last rnd. Slightly gather up stitches evenly around.

MOUNTING MATERIALS:
Masonite or Plywood Circle (¼″ width) — cut to a diam. ¼″ smaller than diam. of seat opening
Staple Gun and ¼″ staples (for Masonite) or Hammer and ¼″ tacks (for plywood)
Polyurethane Foam (1″ thick — available by the yard) — a piece slightly larger than Masonite circle

Muslin — cut 5″ larger all around than Masonite
Sharp Razor Blade
Needle and Sewing Thread

NOTE: If Masonite is used, a staple gun is necessary to penetrate its hard composition. If plywood is used, you can work with tacks instead.

Mounting

1. Cut foam circle: Lay Masonite circle over foam and with razor blade cut through foam, around edge of board.
2. Make knife edge on foam: Pinching side edges of foam together, sew around with needle and thread in overcast stitch.
3. Place foam circle over center of muslin, then place Masonite circle evenly over foam.
4. Bringing muslin over edge of board to wrong side, staple muslin to Masonite ½″ from edge, placing staples about ½″ apart. Stretch muslin tightly throughout. To start, insert 1 staple then staple opposite side. Place next staple halfway between the first 2 staples then staple opposite side. Staple remaining areas between the 4 initial staples.
5. Trim excess muslin.

Assembly: Place crochet cover over seat and gather up stitches with drawstring on back until snug. Tie in a long bow and tuck strands under edge of cover — do not cut drawstring. Extra length is needed when cover is removed for cleaning. Place seat on chair. Seat does not have to be fastened to chair frame; rim will hold it in place.

Cleaning: Untie drawstring and remove cover. Cover can be washed (see washing instructions on p. 142) or dry-cleaned (see dry cleaning information on p. 142).

Chair Cushion

Color Photograph, p. 54

Making a cushion is not difficult, even though there are a number of steps involved. First, a paper pattern is made in the shape of the chair seat and is used to cut out the crocheted fabric for the top and a piece of cloth fabric for the bottom. After the two pieces are sewn together, crocheted piping is tacked around the seam, then the cover is stuffed with a pillow form. The cloth side on the bottom has a zipper across the middle for easy access. The tie-strings are optional depending on furniture style. The crocheted fabric is worked in cotton thread with three colors, forming a striped pattern which can run either vertically or horizontally.

To inspire you, here's a list of furniture items that look well with cushions: wicker or wood-frame side chairs and armchairs, rush and cane seat frame chairs, parson's or deacon's benches, piano benches, stools, rocking chairs, and chest seats. A long bench with a series of small cushions tied to the back rungs might appeal as an interesting hallway project.

Maybe you already have a piece around somewhere that could do with a seat lifting, or if you're blessed with good scrounging instincts, you might come across a salvageable bench or chair that would welcome a new coat of paint and a crocheted cushion.

The chair in the photograph, a dismal reject from the basement of a newly decorated hotel, was one of those scrounger's delights. The center support rung was split, but I successfully glued it back together, and a fresh coat of kelly green paint was in itself a transformation. But the added cushion is really the touch that makes it one of my favorite chairs.

CROCHET MATERIALS:

Coats & Clark's Speed-Cro-Sheen Cotton:

Colors shown are Hunter's Green, Tango, and White

As a guide to quantity: 2 balls each of three colors will make a piece of fabric approx. 15″ × 18″; plus 1 ball of one color is needed for tie-strings and piping

Crochet Hook Size 1

GAUGE: 6 sts = 1 inch
11 rows = 2 inches

NOTE: Stripes repeat in the following color sequence: A, B, A, C, B, C — colors shown are Hunter's Green (A), White (B), and Tango (C). Stripes are shown vertically, but they can run in either direction. For vertical stripes, foundation chain determines width of fabric. For horizontal stripes, foundation chain determines length of fabric. Thread ends do not have to be crocheted over or woven back into work. Edges will be discarded when fabric is cut.

Crocheted Fabric

Row 1: With First Color, ch an even number for desired length or width, 1 sc in 2nd ch from hook, * 1 dc in next ch, 1 sc in next ch; repeat from * across. To end: ch 1, cut thread and pull end out through last st to hold.

Row 2: Turn, attach Next Color in first sc, ch 2 — counts as first dc, * 1 sc in next dc, 1 dc in next sc; repeat from * across. Fasten off.

Row 3: Turn, attach Next Color in first dc, 1 sc in same st, * 1 dc in next sc, 1 sc in next dc; repeat from * across ending with 1 sc in top of end ch. Fasten off.

Repeat Rows 2 & 3 for pattern until desired width or length is reached. Either side of fabric can be used. Choose the side you prefer and mark as right side.

Blocking: Block fabric, if necessary, according to blocking instructions on p. 141.

CUSHION MATERIALS:

Backing Fabric (velvet, corduroy, linen, or other suitable fabric)

Matching Zipper — long enough to reach across width at center of cushion to within 1½″ from each side

Matching Sewing Thread

Double-Faced Tape (or looped pieces of masking or cellophane tape)

Brown Wrapping Paper — to make pattern

Sewing Machine

Pillow Form (see Step 12)

Basic Instructions for Making
Custom-Fitted Cushions

1. With a piece of brown wrapping paper (or similar paper) cut a pattern the shape of cushion area on chair seat — plus an additional ¼″ all around. The additional fullness will be taken up when cushion is stuffed.

2. Front: Make a rectangular or square piece of crocheted fabric 1″ wider all around than widest spread of pattern.

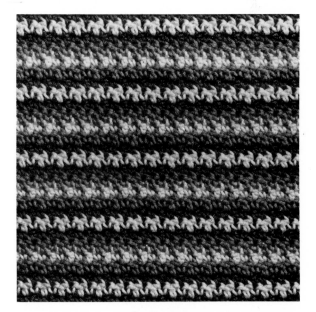

STITCH DETAIL

59

3. With double-faced tape, stick pattern evenly to right side of crocheted fabric. If rows run horizontally, place pattern so that foundation chain edge is at front of seat.

4. To prevent raveling when cutting, set sewing machine at 10 stitches to 1 inch and stitch through crocheted fabric ¼" from edge of pattern — guide side of presser foot around edge of pattern to keep stitching even. Make another row of stitching ¼" from first row toward outside edge, again using presser foot as a guide. Reinforce with another row of stitching over second row.

5. Remove pattern — leave tape on pattern if reusable. Cut crocheted fabric around outside of second stitching row close to stitching.

6. Back: Press backing fabric if wrinkled. Fold fabric in half. Fold pattern evenly in half *crosswise* with tape on outside. (If first tape is not reusable, remove and replace with fresh tape on one half of pattern.) Stick pattern half to backing fabric so there is a 1" fabric allowance around all edges of pattern. With chalk pencil, mark off dots in half-inch intervals around all sides *measuring ⅝" from edge of pattern.* Cut out through both thicknesses on dotted line.

7. Place fabric halves with right sides together corresponding to shape.

8. Make zipper seam: Sew along center edge making a ⅝" seam — use basting stitch across middle portion of seam the length required for zipper. Press seam open. Sew in zipper by hand, or on machine according to package instructions.

9. Tie-Strings (Optional): Figure length of each pair of tie-strings. For each string, crochet a chain this length plus an additional ½". Sl st in 2nd ch from hook and in each ch across. Fasten off with knot. On right side of crocheted fabric, mark each spot with a pin where a pair of tie-strings is desired. Lay tie-strings toward center on right side of crocheted fabric so that knotted ends are even with edges of fabric. Hand-tack to hold. Remove pins.

10. Join Front and Back: Open zipper about 3". Pin Front and Back together with right sides facing. From cloth side, stitch through both thicknesses around ⅝" from edge. To reinforce, make another row of stitching over first row. Clip curved areas of *backing fabric only.* Open zipper all the way and turn to right side. Push out edges and press.

11. Piping: Measure the perimeter of the cushion around seam. Crochet a chain this length plus an additional few inches. Sl st in 2nd ch from hook and in each ch across. Cut thread and pull end out through last st to hold. Start at back of cushion with finished end of piping; with needle and thread hand-sew piping to seam of cushion with overcast stitch. To finish, pull out excess stitches at end of piping and fasten off neatly, tacking the ends together.

12. Pillow Form: Cut 2 pieces of muslin ¾" wider all around than pattern. Make pillow form according to instructions on p. 143. Clip curved edges. Stuff half as full as you normally would for a throw pillow. Place form inside pillow cover and close zipper.

Cleaning: Remove pillow form and have cover dry-cleaned. See p. 142 for dry cleaning information.

Footstool Cushion

Color Photograph, p. 15

The footstool is another little treasure rescued from the dusty degradations of antiquity. The wicker seat was badly torn; so I made a cushion to hide the damages until I had time to have the seat rewoven. I like the cushion so well that I never did bother to get the seat mended.

The cushion shown was crocheted to the shape of the seat. It wasn't until I made the chair cushion that I realized there was an easier way; cutting the crocheted fabric to the desired shape is a lot simpler than working it out with increases and decreases. So assemble the stool cushion the same as the chair cushion on p. 58. The only difference will be in the piping which is shown here as a series of single crochet rows worked on a base of slip stitches that were crocheted around the top edge.

The stitch pattern is a variation on the single crochet decrease worked in six colors of Persian yarn, creating an interesting textured fabric of muted stripes.

61

CROCHET MATERIALS:

Needlepoint Yarn:

As a guide to quantity: 350 total yds. of 6 colors will make a piece of fabric approx. 9″ × 12″

Crochet Hook Size 0

CUSHION MATERIALS:

Same as Chair Cushion on p. 59

GAUGE: 4 sts = 1 inch
5 rows = 1 inch

NOTE: Stripes repeat in the following color sequence: A, B, C, D, E, F, C. Colors shown are Dk. Pink (A), Kelly Green (B), Off-White (C), Lime Green (D), Med. Pink (E), Med. Green (F). Stripes are shown horizontally, but they can run in either direction. For vertical stripes, foundation chain determines width of fabric. For horizontal stripes, foundation chain determines length of fabric. Thread ends do not have to be crocheted over or woven back into work. Edges will be discarded when fabric is cut.

Crocheted Fabric

Row 1: With First Color, make a ch the desired length or width, 1 sc in 2nd ch from hook, * insert hook in same ch as last sc and draw up a loop, insert hook in next ch and draw up a loop, yo and through all 3 loops on hook — joint-sc made; repeat from * across. To end: ch 1, cut yarn and pull end out through last st to hold.

Row 2: Turn, attach Next Color in first st, 1 sc in same st, * insert hook in same st as last sc and draw up a loop, insert hook in next st and draw up a loop, yo and through all 3 loops on hook; repeat from * across. Fasten off.

Repeat Row 2 for pattern until desired width or length is reached. Either side of fabric can be used. Choose the side you prefer and mark as right side.

Blocking: Block fabric, if necessary, according to blocking instructions on p. 141.

Cushion Assembly: See p. 59 for cushion instructions.

Cleaning: Remove pillow form and have cover dry-cleaned. See dry cleaning information on p. 142.

STITCH DETAIL

Upholstered Bench

Color Photograph, p. 66

The bench is yet another salvaged rehabilitation. The oriental borders clearly demanded Chinese red enamel, but the crocheted design took longer thought. I wanted something dramatic but not too complicated to carry out the oriental theme and finally decided on a Chinese longevity symbol. The simplicity of the design, and the tonal qualities between the dark green and light aqua of the fabric against the bright red frame, produced the strong but understated feeling I wanted to capture.

The fabric is worked in cotton with the single crochet jacquard method to simulate needlepoint — an upholstery technique, I might add, that stands in its own right. Just about any charted design can be used, depending on size and suitability.

The upholstery instructions are for furniture pieces with slip seats, the type of seat that is removable — a padded wood frame attached with screws. Larger upholstery projects are involved operations, requiring a great deal of technical know-how, and are best left to professionals.

First, a pattern of the seat is made and the design is crocheted into a rectangular piece of fabric slightly larger than the pattern. Then the fabric is cut to shape and tacked to the seat in regular upholstery fashion. The jacquard technique is just one idea for furniture upholstery. You can use any one of the preceding striped fabrics too.

The braid is optional. The use of trims depends on furniture style. On the bench it was a nice touch; other pieces may look better without it. You may even prefer to use upholstery tacks or commercial trims.

CROCHET MATERIALS:
Coats & Clark's Speed-Cro-Sheen Cotton:
As a guide to quantity: 2 balls of Killarney Green and 9 balls of Aqua will make a piece of fabric approx. 20″ × 30″; plus 1 ball of Green for trim
Crochet Hook Size 1

GAUGE: 6 sc = 1 inch
7 rows = 1 inch

NOTE: Before starting, refer to p. 145 for instructions on how to work jacquard crochet. Fabric is worked with the single crochet method. Each square on the chart = 1 sc.

Crocheted Fabric
To center a design within the dimensions of the finished fabric, first determine size of fabric as in Steps 2 & 3 of Mounting Instructions. Make a foundation chain the desired length. Work a row of sc across chain (for design with an uneven number of stitches, work an uneven number of sc). Subtract the number of stitches in the design (61 stitches in accompanying design) from the number of sc and divide in half. This will be the additional number of stitches you will have to make at each side of the charted stitches (left and right), and must be counted when reading the chart. By computing the row gauge to inches, figure out how many additional rows have to be made at each end of chart (top and bottom) to obtain the proper width. Work first pattern row of design on right side of work. Weave in all thread ends on wrong side.

Braid Trim (Optional)
Row 1: Ch 3, 1 sc in 2nd ch from hook and in next ch.
Row 2: Ch 1, turn, 1 sc in each sc.
Repeat Row 2 until braid is desired length. Braid can be used as is or with added edging to make it wider (as shown).
Edging: Working along edge of rows from *left to right,* work in reverse sc as follows: attach thread in first row, 1 sc in same row, * ch 1, *working toward right* sk 1 row, insert hook in next row, *hook over yarn* and draw up a loop, yo and through both loops on hook; repeat from * across. Fasten off — right side. From right side work across other edge the same. Braid can be glued, sewn, or pinned in place. I prefer the pins; they're easy to remove for cleaning. Use regular straight pins with flat heads. Push pins through edge of braid all the way into bottom edge of seat padding at about 1″ intervals. They will barely show.

MOUNTING MATERIALS:
Sewing Machine
Double-Faced Tape (or looped pieces of masking or cellophane tape)
Brown Wrapping Paper — to make pattern
Black or White Muslin — to cover underside of seat
Hammer and ¼″ Tacks
Straight Pins

Mounting — Basic Instructions for Covering a Slip Seat
1. Remove old upholstery down to muslin cover. If you reupholster over old fabric, the seat enlarges with each new covering and may not fit properly.
2. Make a pattern: Place seat with padded side up on a piece of brown wrapping paper and draw outline of seat. Add 1¼″ around all sides. Cut out.
3. Make a rectangular piece of crocheted fabric large enough to cover pattern plus 1″ all around.
4. With tape, stick pattern to wrong side of crocheted fabric, centering design. If rows run horizontally, place pattern so that foundation chain edge is at front of seat.
5. To prevent raveling when cutting, set sewing machine at 10 stitches to 1 inch and stitch through fabric around edge of pattern. Make another row of stitching ¼″ from first row toward outside edge, guiding presser foot around edge of first row to keep stitching even. Reinforce with another row of stitching over second row.
6. Remove pattern. Cut fabric around outside of second row close to stitching.
7. Place fabric evenly on seat and stick several

pins into the padding at the center and around the edges to hold fabric in place.

8. Gently turn the seat over and tack fabric to wood frame as follows: Tacks should be placed ½″ in from edge at about 1″ intervals all around. Tack the center of each side first, then place a tack about 2″ from each corner on each side. Tack areas between tacks. Do not stretch fabric as you tack. Turn the seat over occasionally to make sure you're not pulling rows unevenly.

Corners: At rounded corners ease in the fullness. For angular corners there is too much bulk if fabric is turned under. After experimenting with various possibilities, I decided on the following mitering method. Hold both sides of the corner fabric together perpendicular to the frame and diagonally in line with corner point, so that surrounding fabric fits snugly against the frame. With needle and thread, stitch pieces together in a diagonal line close to frame to within ⅜″ from corner point. Reinforce with a second row of stitching over first row. Cut excess fabric close to stitches. Reinforce again with overcast stitches across raw ends. Tack in place.

If fabric should cover screw holes in frame, relocate holes by placing the seat in correct position on furniture frame. From underneath, insert a long nail through hole in furniture frame. If seat is aligned properly, nail will go right through hole in seat with a few twists. Work nail in a circular motion to widen fabric around hole.

9. Cover bottom of the seat with a piece of muslin, using fewer tacks. Use pattern to cut out muslin and turn edges under to fit. Muslin should overlap tacks of crocheted fabric and should be stretched taut but not tight. Fastening screws will easily pierce muslin.

10. Fasten seat to furniture frame.

Cleaning: Since the fabric is handmade and represents a good many hours of love and labor, it isn't the sort of thing you merely pull off and replace with a fresh piece. If carefully cared for, cleaning will not be frequent, but when the time comes the fabric has to be removed, which means undoing the trim and carefully removing the tacks. Have the fabric dry-cleaned (see p. 142 for dry cleaning information) and remount.

START PATTERN (RIGHT SIDE)

☐ AQUA   ■ KILARNEY GREEN

5. Pictures

This section is devoted exclusively to "crochet trivia"—
amusing diversions to make just for the fun of it, to hang in
the nooks and crannies.

Bouquet of Crochet

Color Photograph, p. 67

Here's a way to gather a basket of wild flowers and keep them blooming forever. It's all crocheted with embroidery floss and glued on a patch of fresh country gingham. If you prefer yours under glass, mount it in a shadow box frame for true old-fashioned flavor.

As an alternate arrangement, basket and flowers can be tacked to a throw pillow for an embroidered look.

SIZE: 11″ × 11″ Frame Opening

CROCHET MATERIALS:
6-strand Embroidery Floss (9 yd. skeins):
  2 skeins each of Dk. Yellow, Lt. Blue, Lt. Pink, White, Med. Green, and Dk. Green
  3 skeins each of Royal Blue, Red, and Lt. Yellow
  7 skeins Lt. Brown

Alternate: Coats & Clark's Knit-Cro-Sheen Cotton or Pearl Cotton
Crochet Hook Size 7

GAUGE: Basket measures approx. 7¼″ across at widest spread and 4½″ from top to bottom at center.

NOTE: Work tightly for best results.

69

Basket

Row 1 (Right Side): With Lt. Brown, ch 25, work 1 dc in 4th ch from hook and in each ch across — 23 dc counting beginning ch-3 as first dc.

Row 2: Turn, sl st in first dc, ch 2 — counts as first dc, 1 dc in next dc, * ch 1, sk next st, 1 dc in each of next 2 sts; repeat from * across working last dc in top of ch-3.

Row 3: Turn, sl st in first dc, ch 2, 1 dc in same dc as sl st, ch 2, 2 dc in next dc — first shell, * 2 dc in next dc, ch 2, 2 dc in next dc — next shell; repeat from * across working last 2 dc in top of ch-2 — 8 shells.

Row 4: Turn, sl st in each of first 2 dc and in ch-2 space, ch 2, work 1 dc, ch 2, 2 dc all in same space — first shell, * ch 1, work 2 dc, ch 2, 2 dc all in ch-2 space of next shell; repeat from * across.

Rows 5 & 6: Repeat Row 4 twice.

Rows 7 & 8: Repeat Row 4 twice *except* work ch 2 between shells.

Rows 9 & 10: Repeat Row 4 twice *except* work ch 3 between shells.

Rows 11 & 12: Repeat Row 4 twice *except* work ch 4 between shells — Row 12 ends on wrong side. Put loop of last st on safety pin to hold, drop work temporarily and work bottom.

Bottom — Row 1: Working in single loops on opposite side of foundation chain, from right side attach new strand in first ch, 1 sc in same ch, 1 hdc in each of next 2 ch, 1 dc in each of next 2 ch, 1 tr in each of next 5 ch, dec as follows: work 1 tr in next ch working off loops until 2 loops remain on hook, work 1 tr in next ch working off loops until 3 loops remain on hook, yo and through all 3 loops, 1 tr in each of next 6 ch, 1 dc in each of next 2 ch, 1 hdc in each of next 2 ch, 1 sc in last ch.

Row 2: Ch 1, turn, 1 sc in each st across — 22 sc.

Row 3: Ch 1, turn, 1 sc in first sc, * ch 3, sk 2 sts, 1 sc in next sc; repeat from * across — 7 loops.

Row 4: Turn, sl st in first sc, ch 2, work 2 dc, ch 2, 2 dc all over first loop — shell, * 1 sc over next loop, work shell over next loop; repeat from * across, 1 dc in last sc — 4 shells. Fasten off.

Border: From wrong side pick up dropped stitch at top and continue as follows: Ch 1, turn, 1 sc in first dc, ch 3, 1 sc in next dc, (ch 3, 1 sc in ch-2 space) twice, (ch 3, 1 sc in next dc) twice, * working on wrong side of ch, work 1 sc in each of next 4 ch, 1 sc in next dc, ch 3, 1 sc in next dc, (ch 3, 1 sc in ch-2 space) twice, (ch 3, 1 sc in next dc) twice; repeat from * across working last sc in top of ch-2. Working across first side, * ch 3, sl st in 3rd ch from hook — picot, ch 1, 1 sc over end dc of next shell; repeat from * 8 times, work picot, ch 1, 1 sc over end dc of next row, work picot, ch 1, sk next row, 1 sc in end sc of sc-row, ch 3. Working across lower edge, work 1 sc over end dc of next shell, ch 3, 1 sc in top of same dc, (ch 3, 1 sc in next dc) twice, (ch 3, 1 sc in ch-2 space) twice, (ch 3, 1 sc in next dc) twice, * sk next sc, 1 sc in next dc, ch 3, 1 sc in next dc, (ch 3, 1 sc in ch-2 space) twice, (ch 3, 1 sc in next dc) twice; repeat from * twice, ch 3, 1 sc in top of ch-2. Working across second side, ch 3, 1 sc over end dc of same shell, ch 3, 1 sc in end sc of sc-row, work picot, ch 1, sk next row, 1 sc over last dc of dc-row, ** work picot, ch 1, 1 sc over end dc of next shell; repeat from ** 8 times, work picot, ch 1, join with sl st to first sc of first shell. Fasten off.

Handle — Row 1 (Wrong Side): Ch 4, work 1 dc, ch 2, 2 dc in 4th ch from hook — first shell.

Row 2: Turn, sl st in each of first 2 dc and in ch-2 space, ch 2, work 1 dc, ch 2, 2 dc all in same space — next shell.

Repeat Row 2 for total of 40 shells ending on right side. *Do not break thread.* Handle measures approx. 11″.

Handle Border (Worked on one side of shells only):
Do not turn, working along edge of shell rows * work picot, ch 1, 1 sc over end dc of next shell; repeat from * across. Fasten off.

Flowers and Leaves

Note: All are worked from right side — Rnd 1 is always right side. Ends of thread can be tied together in knots on wrong side.

White Flower (Make 4)

Rnd 1 — Center: With Lt. Yellow, ch 2, work 8 sc in 2nd ch from hook, join with sl st to first sc. Fasten off.

Rnd 2 — Petals: Attach White with sl st in any sc, (ch 8, sl st in same sc) twice, * ch 8, sl st in next sc, ch 8, sl st in same sc; repeat from * around — 16 petals. Fasten off.

Large Blue Flower (Make 3)

Rnd 1 — Center: With Dk. Yellow, ch 1 loosely for center, ch 3 more — counts as first dc, work 11 dc in center ch, join with sl st to top of ch-3 — 12 dc. Fasten off.

Rnd 2 — Petals: Attach Royal Blue with sl st in any dc, * ch 7, 1 sc in 2nd ch from hook; working 1 st in each ch, work 1 hdc, 2 dc, 1 hdc and 1 sc in last ch, sl st in next dc of Center; repeat from * around, join last petal with sl st in beginning dc — 12 petals. Fasten off.

Red Flower (Make 3)

Note: Do not join rnds — place a marker in first sc of each rnd.

Base — Rnd 1: With Red, ch 2, work 6 sc in 2nd ch from hook.

Rnd 2: Working in *back loop only,* work 2 sc in each sc around — 12 sc.

Rnd 3: * Working in *back loop,* work 2 sc in next sc, 1 sc in next sc; repeat from * around, join with sl st in back loop of next sc — 18 sc. Fasten off.

Front Side: Working in *front loops* of Base sts, attach Red in beginning sc at center, work 1 sc, ch 2, 1 sc all in same st, * ch 2, work 1 sc in next st, ch 2, work 1 sc, ch 2, 1 sc all in next st; repeat from * around all 3 rnds of Base, join with sl st in same loop as last join. Fasten off.

Large Yellow Flower (Make 3)

Rnd 1 — Center: With Dk. Yellow, ch 1 loosely for center, ch 3 more — counts as first dc, work 11 dc in center ch, join with sl st to *front loop* of 3rd ch at start — 12 dc. *Do not break thread.*

Rnd 2 — Center Petals: Ch 1, work 1 sc, ch 1, 1 sc all in same loop of ch, * ch 1, work 1 sc, ch 1, 1 sc all in *front loop* of next dc; repeat from * around, ch 1, join with sl st in both loops of first sc. Fasten off.

Rnd 3 — Outer Petals: Holding Center Petals forward, attach Lt. Yellow with sl st in *back loop* of ch-3 at beginning of Rnd 1, (ch 6, sl st in 3rd ch from hook — picot, ch 3, sl st in same loop) twice, * ch 6, work picot, ch 3, sl st in *back loop* of next st, ch 6, work picot, ch 3, sl st in *back loop* of same st; repeat from * around — 24 petals. Fasten off. Fluff up Center Petals.

Six-Petal Flower

Make: 2 with Lt. Yellow Center and Lt. Pink Petals
      1 with Lt. Yellow Center and Lt. Blue Petals
      1 with Dk. Yellow Center and Lt. Yellow Petals

Rnd 1 — Center: With Center Color, ch 2, work 6 sc in 2nd ch from hook, join with sl st to first sc. Fasten off.

Rnd 2 — Petals: Attach Petal Color with sl st in any sc, ch 3, 2 dc in same st, ch 2, sl st in next sc, * ch 2, 2 dc in same st, ch 2, sl st in next sc; repeat from * around, end last petal with sl st in same sc — 6 petals. Fasten off.

Small Flower

Make: 2 with Dk. Yellow Center and Lt. Yellow Petals
      4 with Lt. Yellow Center and Lt. Blue Petals
      5 with Lt. Yellow Center and Lt. Pink Petals

Rnd 1 — Center: With Center Color, ch 2, work 6 sc in 2nd ch from hook, join with sl st to first sc. Fasten off.

Rnd 2 — Petals: Attach Petal Color with sl st in any sc, (ch 3, sl st in same sc) twice, * ch 3, sl st in next sc, ch 3, sl st in same sc; repeat from * around — 12 petals. Fasten off.

Double Leaf (Make 5 Dk. Green and 6 Med. Green)

First Leaf: Ch 10, work 1 sc in 2nd ch from hook; working 1 st in each ch, work 1 hdc, 1 dc, 3 tr, 1 dc, 1 hdc and 1 sc in last ch. *Do not break thread.*

Second Leaf: Repeat First Leaf, join with sl st to first ch of First Leaf. Fasten off by tying ends together with double knot. Cut ends close to knot.

Blocking: Lay basket right side up on pressing board. Pin to given measurements smoothing out stitches. Curve handle so that picots are at outer edge. Place handle ends under top edge of basket between 2nd and 3rd shells from each side. Measurement from top of handle to bottom of basket is approx 8½". Pin in place. Steam lightly with moderately hot steam iron, *taking care not to let iron touch work.* Let dry thoroughly before removing. Flowers and leaves should not be blocked.

FRAMING MATERIALS:

Square Frame with 11″ × 11″ opening
White Mat Board (for mounting) — cut to fit frame
Blue Gingham Fabric (¼″ checks) — cut to extend 1″ over all edges of board
White Craft Glue, Flat Paintbrush, Toothpick, and Straight Pins

Assembly

1. Iron fabric, if wrinkled.

2. Dilute glue slightly with water. Brush glue over entire surface of mounting board. Lay fabric wrong side up. Place board evenly on fabric with glue side down. Turn over and smooth out puckers.

3. When dry, trim excess fabric even with board. (If board warps, let it rest under a couple of heavy books for a few hours.)

4. Center basket and handle on fabric, arranging pieces same as for blocking. Hold in place with pins.

5. With a toothpick carefully dab glue on wrong side around edges of basket and handle, pressing in place as you go.

6. Arrange flowers and leaves as shown in color photograph on p. 67. Hold in place with pins. Glue flowers and leaves at center only. Let dry thoroughly and frame.

Strawberry

Color Photograph, p. 67

We seem to be passing through a phase of favorite things — a special motif that irresistably goes to your heart along with an inexplicable urge to collect as many as you can.

I have a friend with an owl urge. Anything owlish cannot be passed up even if necessitating no lunch for three days. Another friend, not quite as self-denying, has a strong frog urge along with a penchant for "miniaturisms." The unique combination inevitably results in such quaint possessions as amphibian petit points and minute renderings of aquatic squiggles closely resembling tadpoles. Butterfly and ladybug people are just as bad, as are the mushroom and elephant collectors.

My urge is strawberries. From saltshakers to needlepoints — and including the edibles — I am hopelessly incurable. And now a crocheted one, worked in single crochet jacquard with embroidery floss — to share with those of you who might have just discovered the same mysterious craving.

SIZE: Crocheted piece is approx. 3½″ × 3½″

CROCHET MATERIALS:
   6-strand Embroidery Floss (9 yd. skeins):
     1 skein each of Red, Yellow, and Kelly Green
     3 skeins White
   Crochet Hook Size 3
   Tapestry Needle #19

GAUGE: 8 sc = 1 inch
         9 rows = 1 inch

NOTE: Before starting, refer to p. 145 for instructions on how to work jacquard crochet. Strawberry is worked with single crochet method. Each square on chart = 1 sc.

To Start — Row 1 (Right Side): With White, ch 30, work 1 sc in 2nd ch from hook and in each ch across — 29 sc.
Row 2: Ch 1, turn, work 1 sc in each sc across. Follow chart for remainder of work. Pattern starts with Row 5 on right side of work.

Blocking: Pin work evenly to pressing board with wrong side up. Steam lightly with moderately hot steam iron, *taking care not to let iron touch work.* Let dry thoroughly before removing.

FRAMING MATERIALS:
   Square Frame (with glass) with 5″ × 5″ opening
   Black Framing Mat — cut to fit frame with
     3″ × 3″ opening
   Masking Tape

Mounting
1. On wrong side of crocheted square, place masking tape diagonally across each corner so that tape ends extend about ½″ from work. Turn to right side.
2. Center framing mat over crocheted piece and press at corners to secure tape.
3. Frame under glass to prevent work from getting soiled.
4. Cut a peice of cardboard to fit frame opening and insert at back. Fasten with small nails at back of cardboard.

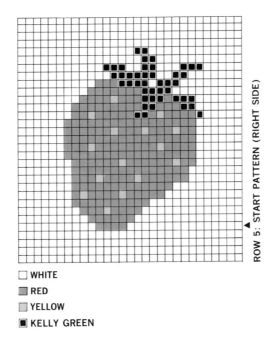

ROW 5: START PATTERN (RIGHT SIDE)

☐ WHITE
▧ RED
▥ YELLOW
■ KELLY GREEN

73

"Love"

Color Photograph, p. 78

For those of you who relegate filet crochet to bedroom bureau covers, here's some friendly persuasion to update your thinking — a crocheted version of the popular "Love" motif, brightly spelled out in Gothic script with red cotton thread and framed in contemporary chrome.

SIZE: Crocheted piece is approx. 8¼″ × 6¼″

CROCHET MATERIALS:
    Coats & Clark's Knit-Cro-Sheen Cotton:
      1 ball Spanish Red
    Crochet Hook Size 9

GAUGE: 4 horizontal or vertical squares = 1 inch

NOTE: Before starting, refer to p. 150 for instructions on how to work filet crochet.

To Start — Row 1 (Right Side): Ch 104, 1 dc in 8th

ch from hook, * sk 2 ch, 1 dc in next ch; repeat from * across — 33 spaces.

Row 2: Ch 5, turn, sk first space, 1 dc in next dc, * ch 2, 1 dc in next dc; repeat from * across working last dc in 3rd ch at end.

Follow chart for remainder of work.

Blocking: Lay work with wrong side up on pressing board. Pin out evenly. Steam lightly with moderately hot steam iron *taking care not to let iron touch work.* Let dry thoroughly before removing.

FRAMING MATERIALS:

10″ × 8″ Sectional Chrome Frame with Glass

White Mat Board (for mounting) — cut to fit frame

White Framing Mat — cut to fit frame with 7¾″ × 5¾″ opening

Masking Tape — ¾″ width

Mounting

1. Center crocheted piece on mounting board.

2. Carefully tape all sides to board, covering chain edge of work only.

3. Place cut mat on top and frame under glass to prevent work from becoming soiled.

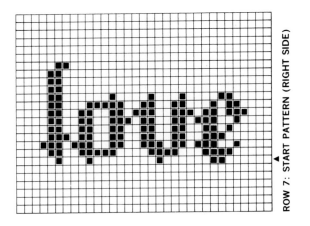

ROW 7: START PATTERN (RIGHT SIDE)

Butterfly

Color Photograph, p. 35

The nostalgia craze has stirred up a lot of attic dust along with a collecting mania unmatched in the recent waves of popular fads. And being no exception to this memorabilia madness, I couldn't resist a crocheted butterfly. Add it to your Lepidoptera collection.

The design is fashioned after a pillowcase edging, dug up in a long-forgotten needlework magazine I once found while on a rummaging rampage through an antique shop. The period frame and ribbon border capture the mood of those "good old days" when handwork was a household pastime and patterns were handed down through the generations.

It's worked with #5 pearl cotton, but Coats & Clark's Knit-Cro-Sheen can be substituted if you like. The Knit-Cro-Sheen is a little thinner so the measurements will be slightly smaller.

Framing directions are included after the crochet instructions. If you prefer a more contemporary arrangement, try gluing the motif on a mirror and mounting it in a sectional chrome frame under glass.

For another variation, the butterfly can be appliquéd to a throw pillow, tacked in place with sewing thread. And I confess to owning a T-shirt sporting a very handsome one made with variegated thread. The random coloring works out exceptionally well.

SIZE: 14″ × 10″ Frame Opening

CROCHET MATERIALS:
  1 ball #5 Pearl Cotton (50 yds.) — Yellow
  Alternate: Coats & Clark's Knit-Cro-Sheen
    Cotton
  Crochet Hook Size 7

GAUGE: Butterfly measures approx. 7″ across
    widest spread of wings. Body is 2½″
    from head to tail.

NOTE: Work tightly for best results.

Body — Row 1 (Right Side): Starting at lower end,
ch 4, 3 dc in 4th ch from hook.
Row 2: Ch 1, turn, 1 sc in next 3 dc, 1 sc in 3rd ch
at end — 4 sc.
Row 3: Ch 1, turn, 1 sc in each sc across (2 sc-rows
form 1 pattern row).
Row 4: Repeat Row 3.
Row 5: Ch 1, turn, 2 sc in first sc, 1 sc in each of
next 2 sc, 2 sc in last sc — 6 sc.
Row 6: Ch 1, turn, 1 sc in each sc across.
Rows 7–19: Repeat Row 6 thirteen times — 9 pattern rows on right side at end of Row 19.
Row 20: Ch 1, turn, dec as follows: insert hook in
first sc and draw up a loop, insert hook in next sc
and draw up a loop, yo and through all 3 loops on
hook, 1 sc in each of next 2 sc, work dec over next
2 sc — 4 sc.
Row 21: Repeat Row 6.
Row 22: Ch 1, turn, work dec over first 2 sc, work
dec over next 2 sc — 2 sc.
Head: Ch 2, turn, work cluster as follows: retaining last loop of each dc on hook, work 2 dc in first
sc and 3 dc in next sc, yo and through all 6 loops
on hook, ch 1 to hold. *Do not break thread.*
Antenna: Ch 25, draw up a loop in 2nd ch from
hook and in next 3 ch, yo and through all 5 loops
on hook, ch 1 to hold. Fasten off. From right side
attach thread in top of cluster toward right of first
antenna, work second antenna the same.

Left Lower Wing — Row 1: With wrong side facing, sk first dc-row and next sc-row at lower end,
attach thread in next row, 1 sc in same row, * ch 5,
sk 1 pattern row, 1 sc in next pattern row * ; repeat
from * to * once, ch 4, sl st in 3rd ch from hook —
picot, ch 2, sk 1 pattern row, 1 sc in next pattern
row; repeat from * to * once — 4 loops.
Row 2: Ch 3, turn (counts as first dc), work 2 dc,
ch 3, 3 dc all over first loop — shell, ch 4, sk picot
loop, (work 3 dc, ch 3, 3 dc all over next loop —
shell) twice.
Row 3: Work picot turning ch as follows: ch 4, sl st
in 3rd ch from hook, ch 2 — turn, work shell in
ch–3 space of first shell ch 4 shell in next shell, ch
1, 7 dc over next ch-4 loop, ch 1, shell in last shell.
Row 4: Work picot turning ch, shell in first shell,
ch 1, sk next ch-1 space, 1 dc in each of next 7 dc
with ch-1 between each dc, ch 1, shell in next
shell, ch 2, 1 sc over center of next loop, ch 2,
shell in last shell.
Row 5: Work picot turning ch, shell in first shell,
ch 3, sk next space, 1 sc in next sc, ch 3, work 3
dc, ch 5, 3 dc all in center of next shell, ch 3, sk
next space, 1 sc between first 2 dc, * ch 3, 1 sc
between next 2 dc; repeat from * 4 times, ch 3,
shell in last shell.
Row 6: Work picot turning ch, shell in first shell,
ch 4, sk next space, 1 sc over next ch-3 loop, * ch
3, 1 sc over next loop; repeat from * 3 times, ch 4,
sk next space, work (3 dc, ch 3) twice and 3 dc all
in center of next shell — double shell, ch 4, sk
next space, 1 sc in next sc, ch 4, shell in last shell.
Row 7: Work picot turning ch, shell in first shell,
ch 5, sk next space, 1 sc in next sc, ch 5, shell in
first ch-3 space of double shell. *Mark next ch-3
space of same shell.*
Row 8: Work picot turning ch, 6 dc in center of
first shell, 1 dc in each of next 3 dc of same shell, 1
dc in each of first 3 dc of next shell, work 3 tr and 3
dtr (yo 3 times) all in center of same shell.
Row 9: Ch 3, turn, sl st in first dtr — picot. Fasten
off.

Left Upper Wing — Row 7: From wrong side attach thread in marked space, ch 3 — counts as first
dc of shell, complete shell in same shell, ch 5, sk
next space, 1 sc over next ch-3 loop, * ch 3, 1 sc
over next loop; repeat from * twice, ch 5, shell in
last shell.
Row 8: Work picot turning ch, shell in first shell,
ch 5, sk next space, 1 sc over next ch-3 loop, * ch
3, 1 sc over next loop; repeat from * once, ch 5,
shell in last shell.
Row 9: Work picot turning ch, shell in first shell,
ch 5, sk next space, 1 sc over next ch-3 loop, ch 3,
1 sc over next loop, ch 5, shell in last shell.
Row 10: Work picot turning ch, shell in first shell,
ch 5, sk next space, 1 sc over ch-3 loop, ch 5, shell
in last shell.
Row 11: Work picot turning ch, shell in first shell,
ch 5, sk next space, 1 sc in sc, ch 5, shell in last
shell.

Row 12: Work picot turning ch, 6 dc in center of first shell, 1 dc in each of next 3 dc of same shell, 1 dc in each of first 3 dc of next shell, 6 dc in center of same shell.

Row 13: Ch 3, turn, sl st in first dc — picot. Fasten off.

Right Wing: With *right side* of body facing, work same as Left Wing. Place sc's of Row 1 to correspond with first side. (*Note: Upper Wing, Row 7, starts with right side facing.*)

Blocking: Lay butterfly right side up on pressing board. Pin out evenly slightly larger than finished measurements. Steam lightly with moderately hot steam iron, *taking care not to let iron touch work.* Let dry thoroughly before removing.

FRAMING MATERIALS:

Frame (with glass) with 14″ × 10″ opening
White Mat Board (for mounting) — cut to fit frame
Fabric (linen, cotton or similar fabric) — cut to extend 1″ over all edges of board
2 yds. Ribbon 1¼″ wide
White Craft Glue, Flat Paintbrush, Toothpick, and Straight Pins

Assembly

1. Iron fabric and ribbon, if wrinkled.
2. Dilute glue slightly with water. Brush glue over entire surface of mounting board. Lay fabric wrong side up. Place board on fabric with glue side down. Turn over and smooth out puckers.

3. When dry, trim excess fabric even with board. (If board warps, let it rest under a couple of heavy books for a few hours.)
4. Cut 2 pieces of ribbon to fit across short sides of board. Spread glue lightly and evenly on wrong side of ribbon and press in place along edge.
5. Cut 2 pieces of ribbon about 5″ longer than long side of board. Lay one piece across one long edge with ends extending equally over sides; hold in place with straight pins. Miter corners as follows: Turn one end of ribbon under to form a right angle,

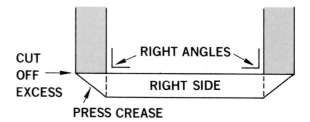

remove ribbon and press crease with iron. Glue wrong sides of ribbon together at overlap; when dry, trim excess turn-under. Lay ribbon in position again and miter opposite end, aligning corners with ribbon on short sides; glue in place. Work other long side the same.
6. Center butterfly on fabric and hold in place with pins. Using a toothpick, carefully dab glue on wrong side around the edges of butterfly, pressing in place with fingers as you go along. Let dry thoroughly and frame. Frame under glass to prevent work from becoming soiled.

6. Pillows

I assume there must be natural boundaries within one's living space that dictate a limit to the number of throw pillows one can comfortably live with, but my rule of thumb is more or less formulated on the principle: As long as you can still sit down on a sofa with ten throw pillows, the pillows stay. Perhaps my own point of saturation extends beyond normal endurance, but on viewing the lifestyles of numerous friends and acquaintances, I have observed that the condition is not uncommon.

Amid all the creative energy stirred up by our renewed zest for things handmade, pillows are one of the most popular expressions of stitchery prowess. Aside from being small works of art in themselves, a hand-crafted pillow tucked in the corner of a chair — or several lined across a sofa — gives furniture added personal charm while providing a convenient setting for displaying one's creative skills.

The pillows that follow vary in size and shape from the delicate, lacy boudoir flounce to the giant-size, rough-textured floor pillows. Most covers are designed with zipper or button closings for easy cleaning. Instructions include the steps for making your own muslin pillow form so you can do all the finishing yourself.

Owl

Color Photograph, p. 79

Children will love it, but you don't have to be a member of the lollipop set to have an owl of your own. Mine has free run of the house and I don't feel the least bit obliged to offer an explanation. He's wide-eyed, witty, and very wise. He's also reversible — fuzzy on one side and plucked on the other.

SIZE: Approx. 10″ × 10″ at widest spread

MATERIALS:
  4-ply Knitting Worsted:
    1 oz. each of Dk. Brown, Yellow, and Lime Green
    4 oz. Orange
  Crochet Hook Size F
  Tapestry Needle #17
  Polyester Fiber Filling for stuffing

NOTE: Work tightly for best results. Do not remove markers until indicated. See p. 141 for helpful hint on working over joinings.

Front — Right Eye
Gauge: Eye is approx. 3½″ across widest spread
Note: All rnds are worked from right side.
Rnd 1 (Right Side): With Dk. Brown, ch 2, work 8 sc in 2nd ch from hook, join with sl st to first sc. Fasten off.
Rnd 2: Attach Lime Green in any sc as follows: holding yarn at back of work, yo hook, then insert hook in st and under end of yarn, yo and draw up a loop, yo and through both loops on hook — sc made, ch 2 — sc plus ch-2 count as first dc (*Note: Always attach new strand in this manner*), work 1 dc in same sc, 2 dc in next sc, 4 tr in each of next 2 sc, 2 dc in each of next 4 sc, join with sl st to top of ch-2 — 20 sts. Fasten off.
Rnd 3: Attach Yellow in 2nd dc after last tr — sc made, ch 2, work 1 dc in same dc, 2 dc in each of next 10 dc, 2 tr in each of next 8 tr, 2 dc in last dc, join with sl st to top of ch-2 — 40 sts. Fasten off.
Rnd 4: Attach Dk. Brown in first tr — sc made, work 1 sc in next st, * 2 sc in next st, 1 sc in each of next 2 sts; repeat from * 4 times, 1 sc in each remaining st, join with sl st to first sc — 45 sts. Fasten off.
From right side, counting toward left and counting first sc of last rnd as first st, place single marker in the 28th sc and double marker in the 34th sc.

Left Eye: Work same as Right Eye, placing double marker in the 33rd sc and single marker in the 39th sc.

Sew Eyes Together: Matching markers, sew the 7 sts from marker to marker together with overcast stitch (see overcast stitch diagram on p. 143). With Dk. Brown and tapestry needle sew from right side through *both loops* of each st, beginning and ending in marked sts.

Beak
Note: All rnds are worked from right side.
Rnd 1: With Yellow, ch 9, work 2 sc in 2nd ch from hook, 1 hdc in next ch, 1 dc in each of next 2 ch, 2 tr in next ch, 1 dc in next ch, 1 hdc in next ch, 3 sc in last ch; working along opposite side of foundation chain work 1 hdc in next ch, 1 dc in next ch, 2 tr in next ch, 1 dc in each of next 2 ch, 1 hdc in next ch, 1 sc in last ch, join with sl st to first sc — lower end. Fasten off.
Rnd 2: Attach Dk. Brown in center sc at lower end — sc made, work 1 more sc in same sc, 1 sc in each of next 4 sts, 2 sc in each of next 2 tr, 1 sc in each of next 3 sts, 3 sc in next st, 1 sc in each of next 3 sts, 2 sc in each of next 2 tr, 1 sc in each of next 4 sts, 1 sc in same sc as first sc, join with sl st to first sc. Fasten off leaving a 5″ strand. Counting from first sc, mark 11th and 19th sc.

Sew Beak to Eyes: On each eye, sk next 3 sts from single marker, place another marker in next st. Place Beak between eyes matching markers. With Dk. Brown, sew Beak in place same as eyes; begin and end in marked sts, match center sc at top of Beak to seam between eyes.

Body
Gauge: 9 dc = 2 inches
        2 rows = 7/8 inch
Attach Orange with sl st in marked st of Right Eye where Beak was joined, ch 7; passing chain under Beak, sl st in corresponding marked st of Left Eye. Fasten off. Remove markers.
Row 1: Hold eyes upside down with right side facing; on Right Eye, counting toward right from st where ch was joined, sk next 8 sts, attach Orange in next st — sc made, ch 2, 1 dc in each of next 7 sts, 1 tr in next st, 1 tr in st where ch is joined, holding Beak forward work 1 tr in each of the 7 ch sts, 1 tr in next st where ch is joined on Left Eye, 1 tr in next st, 1 dc in each of next 8 sts — 27 sts.
Row 2: Turn, sl st in first dc, ch 2 — counts as first dc, work 1 dc in same st — inc, 1 dc in each st across ending with 2 dc in top of ch-2 — inc.
Rows 3–5: Repeat Row 2 three times — 35 sts at end of Row 5.
Row 6: Turn, sl st in first dc, ch 2, work 1 dc in next st and in each st across.

Rows 7 & 8: Repeat Row 6 twice.
Row 9: Turn, sl st in first dc, ch 2, dec as follows: (yo hook, insert hook in next st and draw up a loop, yo and through 2 loops) twice, yo and through all 3 loops on hook — 1 st dec, work 1 dc in each st across to within 3 sts from end, dec over next 2 sts, 1 dc in top of ch-2.
Repeat Row 9 six times — 21 sts at end of last repeat counting each dec as 1 st. Fasten off.

Finish Beak: From wrong side insert hook through center of 17th dc on Row 4 of Body, draw strand at lower end of Beak through to wrong side. Fasten off. With Dk. Brown and tapestry needle, from right side sew Beak to Body working stitches up and down through sc's around edge of Beak. Insert a little stuffing under Beak through opening on wrong side.

Border: With Dk. Brown, sl st around edge of owl as follows: from right side insert hook in any st at bottom, yo and draw up a loop, sl st around *entire* outer edge, working 1 sl st in each dc across bottom, 2 sl sts in the *side* of each dc along edge of rows, and 1 sl st in each sc around eyes.

Fringe: (*Note: See instructions on p. 142 for knotting fringe.*) Wrap Orange around a 2″ piece of cardboard; cut yarn at one edge. Combine 2 strands for each fringe and knot a fringe *around post* of each Orange st. Trim each row evenly.

Back: Work Back same as Front but *do not fringe*. Pieces do not require blocking.

Join Front and Back: Place pieces together with wrong sides facing. With Dk. Brown, crochet from Front side through *both thicknesses,* working in *both loops* of sl sts as follows: starting with matching sts at one corner of lower edge, insert hook in sts, yo and draw up a loop, sl st in each sl st around to within 4″ from start; stop temporarily and stuff pillow until pleasantly plump, pick up dropped loop, and sl st across remaining sts. Fasten off.

Finishing: With Dk. Brown and tapestry needle, tack Front and Back together at top of Beak: insert needle from Back to Front, then through Front to Back; tie ends in single knot drawing sides together. Tie again and fasten off.

Cleaning: Have dry-cleaned. See p. 142 for dry cleaning information.

Giraffe

Color Photograph, p. 79

Here's a bit of whimsy to throw on your sofa or wherever you can squeeze in another pillow — a giraffe donning gold and brown checks to match his checkerboard background. It's worked with knitting worsted in single crochet jacquard; then the front and back are slip stitched together, with a zipper closing.

SIZE: Approx. 11″ × 13″

MATERIALS:
4-ply Knitting Worsted:
   1 oz. each of Lt. Brown, Gold, and Dk. Brown
   4 oz. each of Med. Green and Dk. Green
Crochet Hook Size F
Tapestry Needle #17
9″ Dk. Green Zipper
Needle and Green Sewing Thread
Pillow Form 12″ × 14″ (see p. 85)

GAUGE: 9 sts = 2 inches
              4 rows = ¾ inch

NOTE: Before starting refer to p. 145 for instruc- tions on how to work jacquard crochet. Pillow is worked with single crochet method. Each square on chart = 1 sc.

Front — Row 1 (Wrong Side): With Med. Green, ch 51, work 1 sc in 2nd ch from hook and in each of next 9 ch, complete last sc with Dk. Green; following chart, complete row and remainder of Front. Finished piece is approx. 11″ × 13″.

Blocking: See blocking instructions on p. 141.

Border
Note: On foundation chain edge, work in single loop of each ch.
With right side up, start at right corner of bottom

edge; with Dk. Green, insert hook in first ch and draw up a loop, sl st in each ch across, mark last sl st made — corner. Working across next side along edge of rows, sl st *in between* last 2 sc of rows as follows: sl st in each of first 5 rows, * sk next row, sl st in each of next 4 rows; repeat from * across, sl st in top of first sc, mark last sl st made — 57 sl sts *between* marked sts. Sl st in each sc across top, mark last sl st made — 48 sl sts *between* last 2 marked sts. Working across edge of rows, sl st across same as before, sl st in first ch at start, mark sl st just made — 57 sl sts *between* last 2 marked sts and 48 sl sts *between* marked sts on bottom end. Fasten off.

Back: Work same as Front, working checkerboard background pattern only.

Join Front and Back: Place pieces together with wrong sides facing and matching foundation chain edges; with Dk. Green, crochet pieces together from Front side matching markers at corners, work through *both thicknesses* in *both loops* of each sl st as follows: starting at bottom end, insert hook in 5th st from left corner, yo and draw up a loop, sl st in each sl st around, end in 5th st after right corner on bottom end leaving opening for zipper. Fasten off. With needle and thread sew in zipper.

Pillow Form: Cut 2 pieces of muslin 13″ × 15″ and make pillow form according to instructions on p. 143.

Cleaning: Have cover dry-cleaned. See dry cleaning information on p. 142.

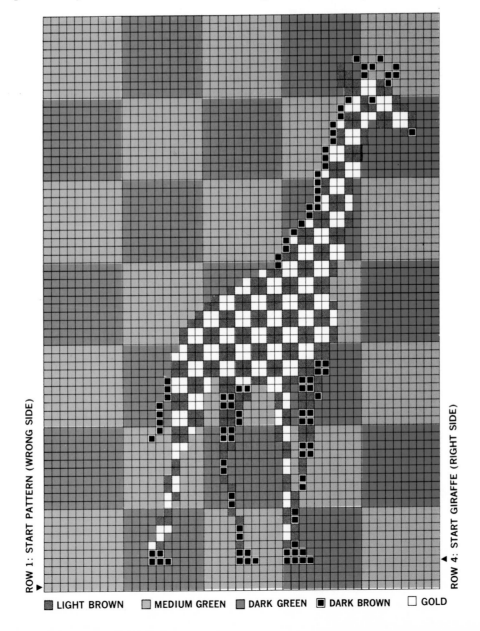

ROW 1: START PATTERN (WRONG SIDE)

ROW 4: START GIRAFFE (RIGHT SIDE)

■ LIGHT BROWN   ■ MEDIUM GREEN   ■ DARK GREEN   ▨ DARK BROWN   □ GOLD

Patch Pillow

Color Photograph, p. 90

One of the advantages of crochet is its natural facility for incorporating other materials. Here a suede patch is used as the center of nine motifs worked in cotton thread and sewn together for the front of a twelve-inch-square throw pillow. For an additional touch, embroidery back-stitching is worked through the holes around each patch.

Patches are available precut and punched, but directions are given for you to make your own from suede, leather, or a wet-look vinyl if you like. Just make sure the material you use can be washed or dry-cleaned.

The back is made in two crocheted sections that overlap, forming an opening so that the cover can be removed. The front and back are crocheted together and bordered in a chain stitch fringe.

SIZE: 12″ × 12″ plus 2″ fringe

MATERIALS:
    Coats & Clark's Speed-Cro-Sheen Cotton:
        1 ball each of Nu-Ecru and Spice
        4 balls Robinette
    Alternate: Lily Double Quick Crochet Cotton
    Crochet Hook Size E
    9 Pink Suede Patches
    Pillow Form — 12″ × 12″ (see p. 88)
    Tapestry Needle #17
    Awl or Leather Punch

Patches: Patches are 2½″ squares with 6 holes punched on each side 10 mm. apart (from center of hole to center of hole). They are usually available in hobby and craft shops, but if you cannot find them, make your own as follows: From a piece of suede or other suitable material, cut nine 2½″ squares. With tracing paper, trace pattern and dots from diagram and cut out. Place pattern over patch aligning edges. With sharp pencil, press through paper on each dot hard enough to leave mark on suede. With a leather punch or awl make holes through dots large enough to insert Size E crochet hook. If using awl, press against a heavy piece of cardboard or sheet of cork. Side from which holes are punched becomes right side of patch.

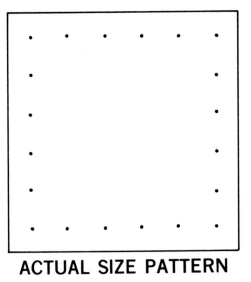

ACTUAL SIZE PATTERN

Front
Gauge: Each motif is a 3¾″ square
Note: All rnds are worked from right side. Crochet over thread ends as you work. See p. 141 for helpful hint on working over joinings.

Motif (Make 9)
Rnd 1: Attach Nu-Ecru in any corner hole of patch as follows: holding thread at back of patch, yo hook, then from right side insert hook in hole and under end of thread, yo and draw up a loop, yo and through both loops on hook — sc made (*Note: Attach all new strands in this manner*), ch 3, 1 sc in same hole — corner, * (ch 1, 1 sc in next hole) 4 times, ch 1, work 1 sc, ch 3, 1 sc all in next hole — corner; repeat from * around ending with 1 sc in last hole before start, ch 1, join with sl st to first sc.
Rnd 2: Ch 1, do not turn, 1 sc in same sc as join, work 1 sc in each ch-1 space and each sc around working 3 sc in each corner space, join with sl st to first sc. Fasten off.
Rnd 3: Attach Robinette in center sc of any corner — sc made, work 2 more sc in same sc, work 1 sc in each sc around working 3 sc in center sc at each corner, join with sl st to first sc. Fasten off.
Rnd 4: With Spice, repeat Rnd 3 — 15 sc *between* 3-sc at corners on each side.

Backstitching (See Diagram): Thread tapestry needle with a 3′ strand of Nu-Ecru. From wrong side insert needle through any hole (A) leaving a 6″ strand at back; go down at B, then up at C; repeat, going down at same hole where last stitch came up. Fasten off by weaving thread ends through stitches on wrong side.

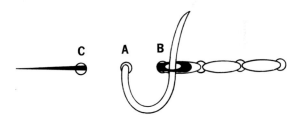

Join Motifs: Sew motifs together to form a square with 3 rows of 3 motifs each. Thread tapestry needle with Spice and sew from right side working overcast stitch (*Note: See p. 143 for overcast stitch diagram*). Insert needle through *both loops* of each sc; start sewing in center sc at one corner and end in center sc at next corner. Work with an even tension to keep seam as elastic as motifs.

Border: From right side attach Spice in center sc at pillow corner — sc made, work 2 more sc in same sc, * 1 sc in each sc across motif ending in first sc of 3-sc at motif corner, 1 hdc in corner sc of same motif, sk seam, 1 hdc in corner sc of next motif; repeat from * across side ending with 3 sc in center sc of next pillow corner, continue around in this manner, join with sl st to first sc — 55 sc *between* 3-sc at corners on each side. Fasten off.

Back
Gauge: 5 sts = 1 inch

       1 dc-row plus 1 sc-row = ⅝ inch

Note: Back is made in 2 sections that overlap at center.

First Half — Row 1 (Right Side): With Robinette, ch 57, work 1 dc in 4th ch from hook and in each ch across — 55 dc counting beginning ch-3 as first dc.

Row 2: Ch 1, turn, 1 sc in each dc across, work last sc in top of ch-3 — 55 sc.

Row 3: Turn, sl st in first sc, ch 3 — counts as first dc, 1 dc in each sc across.

Repeat Rows 2 & 3 for total of 21 rows ending with Row 3. Fasten off.

Border — First Side: From right side attach Robinette in single loop of first ch st of foundation ch — sc made, work 2 more sc in same ch — corner, work 1 sc in single loop of each ch across, end with 3 sc in last ch — 53 sc *between* 3-sc at corners.

Second Side: Working in *side* of sts along edge of rows, work 1 sc in next dc-row, 1 sc in next sc-row, * 2 sc in next dc-row, 1 sc in next sc-row; repeat from * across, end with 1 sc in last dc-row, work 3 sc in top of ch-3 — 30 sc *between* 3-sc at corners. Mark center sc at corner just made; counting back along short side, sk next 9 sts, place a marker in next st.

Third Side: Work 1 sc in each dc across, end with 3 sc in last dc — 53 sc *between* 3-sc at corners. Mark center sc at corner just made.

Fourth Side: Work same as Second Side ending with 1 sc in last dc–row, join with sl st to first sc — 30 sc *between* 3-sc at corners. Fasten off. Counting along short side from st marked at previous corner, sk next 9 sts, place a marker in next st.

Second Half: Work same as First Half.

Join Halves: With right sides up, lay halves long side by long side so that foundation chain edges are on outer sides; at center, lay one half over the other so that short sides overlap 11 sc, matching marked sts; pin each side to hold. From right side attach Spice in center sc at any corner — sc made, work 2 more sc in same sc, work 1 sc in each sc around working 3 sc in center sc at corners and crocheting through *both thicknesses* of 11 sc on each side at overlap; join with sl st to first sc — 55 sc *between* 3-sc at corners on each side. Fasten off.

Join Front and Back: Place Front and Back together with wrong sides facing. *Work through both thicknesses around.* From Front side attach Spice in center sc at any corner — sc made, work 2 more sc in same sc, work 1 sc in each sc around working 3 sc in center sc at each corner, join with sl st to first sc. Fasten off.

Fringe: From Front attach Robinette in any sc — sc made, * ch 20, sl st in next sc; repeat from * around, join with sl st to first sc. Fasten off. Cover does not require blocking.

Pillow Form: Cut 2 pieces of muslin 14″ × 14″ and follow instructions for making pillow form on p. 143. If you prefer, a 12″ square molded form can be used.

Cleaning: If patches are made with suede, have cover dry-cleaned by a suede and leather cleaner. If patches are made with a washable and color-fast fabric, wash according to washing instructions on p. 142; otherwise, have dry-cleaned by a regular dry cleaner. See p. 142 for dry cleaning information. For spot-cleaning suede, a soft pink eraser rubbed over the suede will remove surface soil.

Heart

Color Photograph, p. 91

Red suede and cross stitch embroidery are the center attractions is this valentine pillow. Two hearts are crocheted together with knitting worsted in a rainbow of ruffles. Make it for someone you love.

SIZE: Approx. 11½″ × 11½″

CROCHET MATERIALS:
4-ply Knitting Worsted:
1 oz. each of Med. Orange, Yellow, Lime Green, Lt. Purple, and White
2 oz. each of Red and Royal Blue
Crochet Hook Size F
Tapestry Needle #17

PILLOW MATERIALS:
Red Suede (vinyl, or other suitable nonraveling material) — enough for 2 hearts the size of pattern
Polyester Fiber Filling (for stuffing)
Tracing Paper
Awl or Leather Punch
Double-Faced Tape (or looped pieces of masking or cellophane tape)
Sharp Scissors

Heart (Make 2)

1. With tracing paper, trace heart and dots from pattern. Cut out.

2. Place a few pieces of tape on back of pattern and press to suede. Cut suede around edge of pattern.

3. Mark dots: With pencil, press through each dot on pattern hard enough to leave mark on suede. Remove pattern.

4. With leather punch or awl, punch holes through dots — punch holes around outer edge large enough to insert Size F crochet hook; make center holes for embroidery large enough to insert tapestry needle. Side from which holes are punched becomes right side of heart. (If using awl, press against a piece of heavy cardboard or sheet of cork.)

Embroidery: With tapestry needle work cross stitch in center holes of each heart. Follow numbers on Cross Stitch Diagram for stitch sequence. Make sure stitches all cross in the same direction.

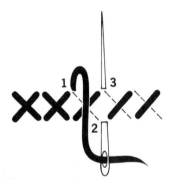

Refer to Placement Diagram for arrangement of colors and stitches.

Border Around Each Heart: From right side attach White in hole at bottom point as follows: holding yarn at back of heart, yo hook, then insert hook in hole and under end of yarn and draw up a loop, yo and through both loops on hook — sc made (*Note: Attach all new strands in this manner*), work 2 more sc in same hole, * work 2 sc in next hole * ; repeat from * to * to "V" at top of heart, end with 2 sc in 2nd hole before center hole, 1 sc in each of next 3 holes; repeat from * to * around 2nd half, join with sl st to first sc. Fasten off.

Join Hearts: Place hearts together with wrong sides facing; work in *both loops* of each st and through *both thicknesses* as follows: attach Lt. Purple in center sc at bottom point — sc made, work 2 more sc in same sc, work 1 sc in each sc to top "V" ending with 1 sc in 2nd sc of last 2-sc group, dec as follows: (insert hook in next sc and draw up a loop) twice, yo and through all 3 loops on hook, work 1 sc in each sc around ending about 3″ from start. Drop work temporarily and stuff pillow. Pick up work and continue with 1 sc in each sc, join with sl st to first sc. Fasten off — *this side is right side of work.*

Ruffle

Note: Attach each new strand away from joining of previous rnd.

Rnd 1: From right side attach Royal Blue in any sc — sc made, ch 3 (sc plus ch-3 count as first tr), ch 1 more, 1 tr in same sc, ch 1, * work (1 tr, ch 1) twice all in next sc; repeat from * around, join with sl st to 3rd ch at start. Fasten off.

Rnd 2: From wrong side, attach Lime Green in any tr — sc made, ch 1, * sk ch, 1 sc in next st, ch

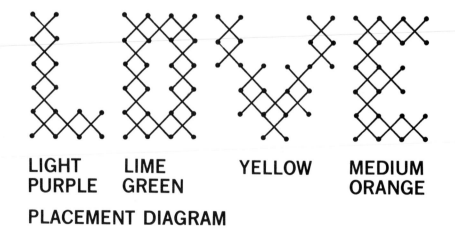

LIGHT PURPLE   **LIME GREEN**   **YELLOW**   **MEDIUM ORANGE**

PLACEMENT DIAGRAM

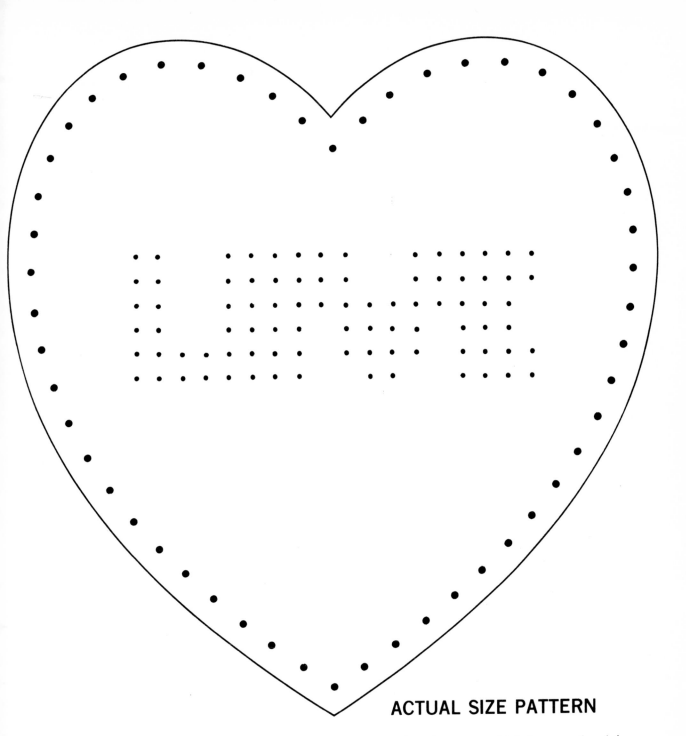

ACTUAL SIZE PATTERN

1; repeat from * around, join with sl st to first sc. Fasten off.

Rnd 3: From right side attach Yellow in any sc — sc made, ch 2 (sc plus ch-2 count as first dc), ch 1 more, * sk ch, 1 dc in next st, ch 1; repeat from * around, join with sl st to 2nd ch at start. Fasten off.

Rnd 4: From wrong side attach Med. Orange in any dc — sc made, continue same as Rnd 2.

Rnd 5: With Red, repeat Rnd 3. *Do not break yarn.*

Edging: Ch 2, do not turn, 1 hdc in same ch as join, sl st in next dc, * ch 2, 1 hdc in same dc, sl st in next dc; repeat from * around, join with sl st to first ch at start. Fasten off.

Cleaning: If heart is made with suede, have pillow dry-cleaned by a suede and leather cleaner; if made with fabric, have dry-cleaned by a regular dry cleaner. See p. 142 for dry cleaning information. For spot-cleaning suede, a soft pink eraser rubbed over the suede will remove surface soil.

93

Floor Pillows

Color Photograph, p. 90

I'm a floor sitter. When the guests arrive, I invariably take to the floor and spend the evening looking up at everybody's chin. It's not a furniture shortage, it's the way I like it. And for those of you who have a similar proclivity for floor lounging, here are two giant pillows to soften the sitting.

Both are made with Reynolds Tapis Pingouin, an acrylic rug yarn that works up quickly into two 2-foot squares of complementary patterns with rich nubby textures. Use them in an overlapping arrangement for a casual lounge or stack them hassock style.

94

FIRST PILLOW (top pillow in photograph)

FINISHED SIZE: Approx. 24″ × 24″

MATERIALS:
Reynolds Tapis Pingouin Rug Yarn (1¾ oz. skeins):
29 skeins Lt. Blue #29
Alternate: Any equivalent weight bulky rug yarn
Crochet Hook Size I
Pillow Form 26″ × 26″

GAUGE: 2 sts = 1 inch
1 dc-row plus 1 sc-row = 1 inch

Front — Row 1 (Right Side): Ch 53, work 1 dc in 4th ch from hook and in each ch across — 51 dc counting turning ch as first dc.
Row 2: Ch 1, turn, 1 sc in each dc across, work last sc in top of end ch — 51 sc.
Row 3: Turn, sl st in first sc, ch 2 — counts as first dc, work 1 dc around post of 2nd dc on 2nd row below inserting hook from front to back to front, * sk 1 sc, 1 dc in next sc, sk 1 dc, 1 dc around post of next dc on 2nd row below; repeat from * across ending with 1 dc in last sc — 51 dc.
Row 4: Repeat Row 2.
Row 5: Turn, sl st in first sc, ch 2, 1 dc in 2nd sc, 1 dc around post of 3rd dc on 2nd row below, * sk 1 sc, 1 dc in next sc, sk 1 dc, 1 dc around post of next dc on 2nd row below; repeat from * across ending with 1 dc in each of last 2 sc.
Repeat Rows 2–5 for pattern for total of 25 dc-rows ending with Row 5. Fasten off. Piece measures approx. 25″ × 25″.

Border
Note: On foundation chain edge, work in single loop of each ch. There will be 49 sl sts between marked sts at corners on all sides.
First Side: From right side insert hook in first ch of foundation chain, yo and draw up a loop, sl st in each ch across, mark last sl st made — corner.
Second Side: Working across edge of rows sl st in space between first and second dc of first row, * sl st in sc of next row, sl st in space between first and second dc of next row; repeat from * across, sl st in top of ch-2, mark sl st just made.
Third Side: Sl st in each dc across top edge, mark last sl st made.
Fourth Side: Work across edge of rows same as Second Side ending with sl st in first ch at start, mark sl st just made. Fasten off.

Back: Work same as Front.

Tassels (Make 4): Wrap yarn 25 times around a 4″ piece of cardboard and make tassels according to instructions on p. 142. Tassels will be attached later.

Pillow Form: Cut 2 pieces of muslin 27″ × 27″ and make pillow form according to instructions on p. 143.

Join Front and Back: Place pieces together with wrong sides facing and foundation chain ends at top. Working in *both loops* of sl sts and matching corners, crochet through *both thicknesses* as follows: insert hook in 4th sl st from left corner on chain end, yo and draw up a loop, sl st in each sl st around ending in 4th st after last corner on chain end, drop work temporarily. Attach a tassel to each corner by drawing tying strands of tassels through sts to wrong side with crochet hook — tie in knot; insert pillow form. Pick up work and sl st across remaining sts. Fasten off so that end can be easily located to reopen side for cleaning.

Cleaning: Remove pillow form and have cover dry-cleaned. See p. 142 for dry cleaning information.

SECOND PILLOW (bottom pillow in photograph)

FINISHED SIZE: Approx. 24″ × 24″

MATERIALS:
Reynolds Tapis Pingouin Rug Yarn (1¾ oz. skeins):
30 skeins Lt. Rose #15
Alternate: Any equivalent weight bulky rug yarn
Crochet Hook Size I
Pillow Form 26″ × 26″

GAUGE: 2 joint-sc = 1 inch
2 rows = ⅞ inch

Front — Row 1 (Right Side): Ch 51, 1 sc in 2nd ch from hook, * insert hook in same ch as last sc and draw up a loop, insert hook in next ch and draw up a loop, yo and through all 3 loops on hook — joint-sc made; repeat from * across — 50 sts.
Row 2: Ch 1, turn, 1 sc in first st, * insert hook in same st as last st and draw up a loop, insert hook in next st and draw up a loop, yo and through all 3 loops on hook; repeat from * across.

95

STITCH DETAIL (TOP PILLOW)

STITCH DETAIL (BOTTOM PILLOW)

Repeat Row 2 for pattern for total of 56 rows. Piece measures approx. 25″ × 25″.

Border
Note: On foundation chain edge, work in single loop of each ch. There will be 48 sl sts between marked sts at corners on all sides.
First Side: From right side insert hook in first ch of foundation chain, yo and draw up a loop, sl st in each ch across, mark last sl st made — corner.
Second Side: Working across edge of rows, * sk next row, sl st in each of next 6 rows; repeat from

* across, sl st in first sc of top edge, mark sl st just made.
Third Side: Sl st in each sc across top edge, mark last sl st made.
Fourth Side: Work across edge of rows same as Second Side ending with sl st in first ch at start, mark sl st just made. Fasten off.

Back: Work same as Front.

Finishing: Make pillow form and tassels and join Front and Back same as First Pillow on p. 95. Same cleaning instructions apply.

Lace Pillow

Color Photograph, p. 23

Indulge your fancy with a little frippery! This double-ruffled pillow sham is a dual ensemble of jacquard and filet crochet stitched into a delicate puff of frills and flowers. It's worked in cotton thread and closed with buttons over a green linen pillow to show off the lacy background.

SIZE: Approx. 14″ × 14″ plus 1½″ ruffle

MATERIALS:
Coats & Clark's Knit-Cro-Sheen Cotton:
1 ball each of Hunter's Green, Chartreuse Green, Skipper Blue, Spanish Red, and Watermelon
7 balls White
Crochet Hook Size 9

12 Buttons — 5/16″ diam.
½ yd. Green Linen Fabric (for pillow form)
Sewing Thread to match
Polyester Fiber Filling (for stuffing)

GAUGE: 4 horizontal or vertical squares = 1 inch

NOTE: Before starting, refer to p. 150 for instructions on how to work filet crochet, and p. 145 for

instructions on how to work jacquard crochet.

Front is worked from two charts simultaneously. One chart is for the jacquard crochet oval containing the flower design, and the other is for the filet crochet background pattern.

The charts are distorted in relation to each other because the squares on one chart represent a different number of stitches from the squares on the other chart. On the Chart for Filet Crochet, each square = 3 sts (either 3 dc for a block or 1 dc plus 2 ch sts for a space). On the Chart for Jacquard Crochet, each square = 2 dc. The rows on both charts are equal.

Front — Row 1 (Right Side): Starting with Chart for Filet Crochet, with White, ch 173, 1 dc in 8th ch from hook, * ch 2, sk 2 ch, 1 dc in next ch; repeat from * across — 56 spaces.

Row 2: Ch 5, turn, sk first space, 1 dc in next dc, * ch 2, 1 dc in next dc; repeat from * across working last dc in 3rd ch at end. Follow Filet Chart through Row 12.

Row 13: Follow Filet Chart across row for 24 squares ending with dc; following Row 13 on Jacquard Chart, * work 2 dc in next space, 1 dc in next dc; repeat from * 7 times — 25 dc; following same row on Filet Chart, work remainder of row to correspond to first side.

Row 14: Follow Filet Chart across row for 22 squares ending with dc; following Row 14 on Jacquard Chart, (work 2 dc in next space, 1 dc in next dc) twice, 1 dc in each of next 24 dc, (2 dc in next space, 1 dc in next dc) twice — 37 dc; following same row on Filet Chart, work remainder of row to correspond to first side. Continue work following both charts through Row 44, which ends the jacquard crochet oval. Follow Filet Chart for remainder of Front.

Center Ruffle

Note: First rnd of ruffle is worked in the sts

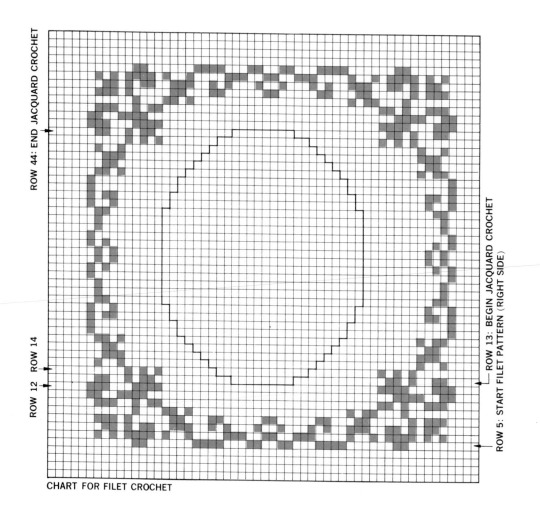

CHART FOR FILET CROCHET

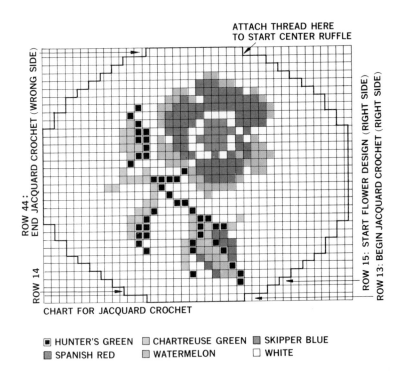

ATTACH THREAD HERE
TO START CENTER RUFFLE

ROW 44:
END JACQUARD CROCHET (WRONG SIDE)

ROW 14

ROW 15: START FLOWER DESIGN (RIGHT SIDE)
ROW 13: BEGIN JACQUARD CROCHET (RIGHT SIDE)

CHART FOR JACQUARD CROCHET

■ HUNTER'S GREEN □ CHARTREUSE GREEN ■ SKIPPER BLUE
■ SPANISH RED ▨ WATERMELON □ WHITE

around edge of jacquard crochet oval. All rnds are worked from right side.

Rnd 1 — Top Edge: From right side attach White over post of first dc at top row of oval (see Jacquard Crochet Chart), ch 5, 1 dc over post of same dc, * ch 2, 1 dc in next dc; repeat from * across (*Note: When working in a dc where another st has already been worked, hold st toward left to insert hook*), end with dc in next to last dc of jacquard row.

First Diagonal Side: Ch 2, 1 dc over post of end dc of same row, ch 2, 1 dc over post of same dc, ch 2, 1 dc in 6th st from end of next row, (ch 2, 1 dc in next dc) 4 times, (ch 2, 1 dc over post of end dc of same row) twice, * ch 2, 1 dc in 3rd st from end of next row, ch 2, 1 dc in next st, (ch 2, 1 dc over post of end dc of same row) twice; repeat from * 3 times, ** ch 2, 1 dc in 3rd st from end of next row, ch 2, 1 dc in next st, (ch 2, 1 dc over post of end dc of same row) twice, ch 2, 1 dc over post of end dc of next row, ch 2, 1 dc over post of same dc; repeat from ** twice.

Straight Side: Work (ch 2, 1 dc over post of end dc of next row, ch 2, 1 dc over post of same dc) 10 times.

Continue working in this manner around remaining sides of oval (*Note: When working in a dc with work upside-down, insert hook under the 2 base loops of each st*) ending with ch-2, join with sl st to 3rd ch at start.

Rnd 2: Ch 5, do not turn, sk first space, 1 dc in next dc, * ch 2, 1 dc in next dc; repeat from * around ending with ch-2, join with sl st to 3rd ch at start.

Rnd 3: Repeat Rnd 2.

Edging: Ch 1, do not turn, 1 sc in same ch as join, ch 2, 1 dc in same ch, * 1 sc in next dc, ch 2, 1 dc in same dc; repeat from * around, join with sl st to first sc. Fasten off.

Back: Work Rows 1 & 2 same as Front. Repeat Row 2 of Front for total of 56 rows. Fasten off. (Or work back in filet pattern following Filet Chart only — work filet mesh across center oval area).

Join Front and Back — First Side: Place pieces with wrong sides facing and with foundation chains on same edge. Hold work with foundation chain at top. Working through *both thicknesses* and working in single loop of foundation chain at base of each dc, from Front side attach White in first dc at right corner, ch 5, work 1 dc, ch 2, 1 dc all in next space, ch 2, 1 dc in next dc, (ch 2, work 1 dc, ch 2, 1 dc all in next space, ch 2, 1 dc in next dc) 5 times, * ch 2, working through *Front side only* for opening work 1 dc, ch 2, 1 dc all in next space, ch 2, 1 dc in next dc; repeat from * across ending in 7th dc from end — count end ch as 1 dc (*Note: Work through both thicknesses for remainder of row*), ** ch 2, work 1 dc, ch 2, 1 dc all in

99

next space, ch 2, 1 dc in next dc; repeat from ** across to corner ending with dc in 3rd ch at corner. **Second Side:** * Ch 2, work 1 dc, ch 2, 1 dc all in same corner space, ch 2, 1 dc in the side of st on next row, * ch 2, work 1 dc, ch 2, 1 dc all in next space, ch 2, 1 dc in the side of st on next row; repeat from * across ending with 1 dc in dc at next corner.

Continue around remaining 2 sides in this manner ending with ch-2, join with sl st to 3rd ch at start. *Do not break thread.*

Outer Ruffle: Repeat Rnd 2 of Center Ruffle for 7 more rows. Work Edging same as Center Ruffle.

Buttons: Sew buttons on wrong side of Front, along edge at base of ruffle. Place first button at 2nd space from end of opening, then sew a button at every 3rd space. Use corresponding spaces on first row of Back as buttonholes.

Pillow Form: Cut 2 pieces of linen 15″ × 15″ and make pillow form according to instructions on p. 143. Cover does not require blocking. Place over pillow and button closed.

Cleaning: Cover can be hand-washed or dry-cleaned (see p. 142 for washing and dry cleaning information).

Moroccan Pillow

Color Photograph, p. 102

If you have a predilection for camels and caftans, here's a throw pillow to add foreign intrigue to your Arabian nights. It's an oasis of exotic colors rippling in bright stripes of single crochets. It works on the floor, on a chair, or a pile of them stacks into a lively tasseled hassock.

SIZE: Approx. 25″ from point to point plus 2½″ tassels

CROCHET MATERIALS:
4-ply Knitting Worsted:
    8 oz. each of Lime Green, Lt. Orange, Red, and Dk. Turquoise
Crochet Hook Size F

GAUGE: 9 sts = 2 inches
            4 rows = 1 inch

NOTE: All rnds are worked from right side. Crochet over yarn ends as you work. When changing colors, attach new strand away from joining of previous rnd. See p. 141 for helpful hint on crocheting over joinings.

Colors: Colors repeat in the following sequence starting with Rnd 5: *1 row each* of Lt. Orange, Lime Green, Red, and Dk. Turquoise. Starting with Rnd 19 (Red), colors repeat in the same sequence with *2 rnds of each color.*

Front — Rnd 1 (Right Side): Starting at center, with Lime Green, ch 2, work 8 sc in 2nd ch from hook, join with sl st to first sc. *Do not break yarn.*

Rnd 2: Work first cluster as follows: ch 2, (yo and insert hook in same sc as join, yo and draw up a loop, yo and through 2 loops on hook) 3 times, yo and through all 4 loops on hook, * ch 3, work next cluster as follows: yo and insert hook in next sc, yo and draw up a loop, yo and through 2 loops on hook (yo and insert hook in same sc, yo and draw up a loop, yo and through 2 loops on hook) 3 times, yo and through all 5 loops on hook; repeat from * 6 times, ch 3, join with sl st to top of first cluster — 8 clusters. Fasten off.

Rnd 3: Attach Red in any space as follows: holding yarn at back of work, yo hook, then insert hook in space and under end of yarn, yo and draw up a loop, yo and through both loops on hook — sc made (*Note: Attach all new strands in this manner*), work 4 more sc in same space, * work 5 sc in next space; repeat from * around, join with sl st to first sc. Fasten off.

Rnd 4: Attach Dk. Turquoise in center sc of any 5-sc group — sc made, work 2 more sc in same st — point, 1 sc in next st, * dec as follows: (insert hook in next sc and draw up a loop) twice, yo and through all 3 loops on hook, 1 sc in next st, 3 sc in next st — point, 1 sc in next st; repeat from * around ending with dec, 1 sc in next st, join with sl st to first sc. Fasten off.

Rnd 5: Attach Next Color in center sc of any point — sc made, work 2 more sc in same st, work 1 sc in each sc around skipping each dec and working 3 sc in center sc at points, join with sl st to first sc. Fasten off.

Rnd 6: Attach Next Color in center sc of any point — sc made, work 2 more sc in same st, work 1 sc in each st around working 3 sc in center sc at points, join with sl st to first sc. Fasten off.

Rnd 7: Attach Next Color in center sc of any point — sc made, work 2 more sc in same st, * 1 sc in each st across ending in sc next to the *2 center sc between points*, work dec over next 2 sts, 1 sc in each st across to next point, 3 sc in center sc of point; repeat from * around ending last repeat with dec, 1 sc in each remaining st, join with sl st to first sc. Fasten off.

Repeat Rnds 5–7 for total of 36 rnds ending with Red. *Start 2 rnds of each color with Rnd 19.*

Back: Work same as Front.

Blocking: See blocking instructions on p. 141.

Center Poms (Make 2 with Dk. Turquoise): Cut a piece of cardboard 2″ wide. Lay a 15″ strand of yarn lengthwise across cardboard. Wind another length of yarn crosswise around cardboard and over strand 80 times. Slip loops off. Tie loops together with the 15″ strand in a secure knot. Cut loops and trim pom to 1¼″. With tying strands, attach a pom to center of each side. Cut tying strands.

PILLOW FORM MATERIALS:
   2 yds. Muslin
   Polyester Fiber Filling (for stuffing)
   #13 Chenille Needle (with sharp point)
   1 yd. Strong Cord

Pillow Form
1. Cut 2 pieces of muslin each 30″ square. Using one piece as pattern, fold as follows to make creases indicated by broken lines in diagram: Creasing each fold tightly, fold square in half and in half again, then fold on the diagonal. Unfold. Make a dot at Center A. Mark a dot on each fold line 13¾″ from Center A.

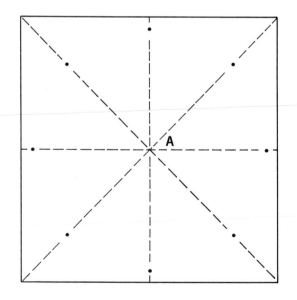

2. Mark a dot evenly spaced between first dots, each 11″ from Center A.

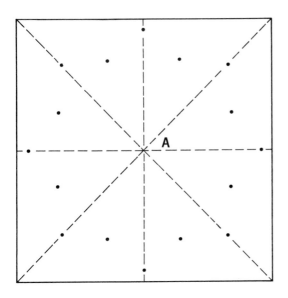

3. Draw connecting lines between dots.

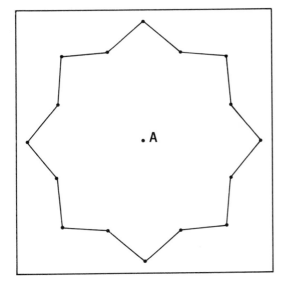

4. Pin the 2 pieces of muslin together and cut out on solid lines. Mark a dot at center of 2nd piece. Marked sides are right sides.

5. Place pieces together with right sides facing. Sew ½″ from edge, leaving both sides of one point open. Reinforce with another row of stitching over first row. Clip corners at "V's" and outer

points. Continue same as pillow form instructions on p. 144 starting with Step 3.

Tuft Pillow Form: Cut cord in half and thread a *double strand* on chenille needle. Insert needle through center dot on one side of pillow and bring out through dot on other side, leaving a 9″ strand on first side; bring needle back through pillow to first side about ⅜″ away from dot — leave needle in place. Tie cord ends together, drawing up centers as close as possible. Knot securely. Bring needle back through to other side so that 2 pieces of cord extend from center on each side of pillow form.

Join Crocheted Pieces: Place pieces together with wrong sides facing and matching points. With Red, crochet through *both thicknesses* working in *both loops* of each sc as follows: insert hook in center sc of any point and draw up a loop, sl st in each st half way around, insert pillow form, sl st around remaining sts, end with sl st in beginning sc. Fasten off so end can be easily located to reopen for cleaning.

Tuft Cover: Using crochet hook, on one side draw up cords from pillow form through 2 opposite spaces at center. Tie ends together, drawing center of cover down to meet pillow form. Knot securely. Do not cut cord — knot has to be untied for cleaning. Stuff cord ends through spaces under the cover. Tuft other side the same.

Tassels (Make 16 with Dk. Turquoise): Wrap yarn around a 2½″ piece of carboard 50 times and make tassels according to instructions on p. 142. Fasten off tying ends securely and cut. Using sewing thread, sew a tassel to each "V" and outer point.

Cleaning: Pillow has to be disassembled for cleaning. Untie tufting cords from center of cover on each side. Remove tassels and pull out slip stitching around one half of cover. Remove pillow form. Have cover and tassels dry-cleaned. See p. 142 for dry cleaning information.

7. Extra Touches

The remaining projects are grouped together as a potpourri. Afghans, curtains, dining accessories, and sundry other crochetables are all collected in a surprise package of house warmers.

Plant Containers

Color Photograph, p. 103

Plant people are known to be extremely loving, excessively doting, overly protective, and passionately devoted when it comes to the care of their botanical charges. If you are part of this eccentric green-thumb contingent, you have probably appropriated everything from bean pots to Great-Grandmother's silver samovar as decorative containers in which to show them off. Some people go for the dramatic flair of unstrung banjos, Victrola horns, and footed bathtubs to house their growing greenery, but for those of you who will settle for the more conventional, here are two crocheted baskets.

The tall container is really a trash can in disguise. A crocheted cover is made to fit over a metal or plastic can with the last few rows turned over the top rim. It's made in continuous rounds of single crochets with the same heavy cord ("Home-Ties" Indoor Line) used as hanging cords for the plant hangers on p. 112. The directions will accommodate any size can; so you might like to make several in different heights and group them together.

The smaller container is also made in continuous rounds of single crochets but worked over rope, which gives it an interesting basket look and enough body to stand on its own. The rope is the ordinary clothesline variety and can be purchased in dime stores and hardware stores, usually packaged in hundred-foot lengths. Some hardware stores carry it reeled on large spools and sell it by the yard. Be sure to get the #7 size. A different diameter will make a difference in the stitch increases of the bottom circle. It's crocheted with a double strand of #15 Cable Cord, also used for making the plant hangers. The directions will accommodate any size.

Plants should not be planted directly in the containers. Pot plants first and set on non-porous saucers, then place inside. The saucer should be deep enough to catch the overflow from watering. Metal cans will rust if water drips to the bottom and will eventually stain the cover and the floor. If you wish, spray the interior of metal cans with a clear acrylic spray. It dries quickly and prevents rust. To elevate plant in a tall container, invert another trash can or bucket (with a smaller diameter) that's about two-thirds the height of the container, and place inside on the bottom. Set the plant and saucer on the up-turned end.

CAN PLANTER

MATERIALS:

January & Wood Co. "Home-Ties" Indoor Line (45 ft. skeins)
  As a guide to quantity: 22 skeins will cover the can shown, which is 9½" in diam. and 18" high
Crochet Hook Size J
Cylindrical Trash Can with straight sides

GAUGE: 2 sts = 1 inch
             2 rows = 1 inch

NOTE: All rnds are worked from right side. Do not join rnds — mark first st of each rnd. Cover should fit snugly over can.

Bottom — Rnd 1 (Right Side): Ch 1 for center drawing up loop to measure 1¼", ch 1 more, work 14 sc in center ch, do not join.
Note: Hereafter, work in back loops of all sts throughout.
Rnd 2: * Work 2 sc in next st — inc, 1 sc in next st; repeat from * around — 21 sc.
Rnd 3: * Work 1 sc in each of next 2 sts, 2 sc in next st; repeat from * around — 28 sc.
Rnd 4: * Work 2 sc in next st, 1 sc in each of next 3 sts; repeat from * around — 35 sc.
Continue in this manner, increasing 7 sc in each

rnd, until circle is desired diameter. Do not inc directly over inc of previous rnd. *Diameter of bottom circle should be about ¾" larger than can diameter.* Remove maker.

Side: Work 1 sc in each st around and around until side is desired height plus 3" more for turn-over. Finish as follows: Sl st in next 3 sts. Fasten off. Place cover over can and turn edge over top rim.

Cleaning: Remove cover and wash according to washing instructions on p. 142. Stuff loosely with newspapers or towels and lay on its side to dry. Let dry thoroughly before replacing over can.

ROPE PLANTER

MATERIALS:

#15 Cable Cord (125 ft. balls) — "Home-Ties", January & Wood Co., or "Gramco", Wm. J. Graham Co.
#7 Clothesline Sash Cord (7⁄32" diam.)
  As a guide to quantity, the basket shown is 9" in diam. and 7" high and requires 8 balls of cable cord and 50 ft. of rope.
Crochet Hook Size J

GAUGE: 2 sts = 1 inch

2 rows = 1 inch

NOTE: Work with double strand of cord throughout. Work in both loops of all sts unless otherwise specified. All rnds are worked from right side. Do not join rnds — mark first st of each rnd.

Bottom — Rnd 1 (Right Side): Ch 1 loosely for center, ch 1 more, work 10 sc in center ch, do not join.

Rnd 2: Holding end of rope at edge of work with cord at front, insert hook in next sc and under rope, yo and draw up a loop to top of rope, yo and through both loops on hook — sc made (*Note: Work sc's over rope throughout, keeping end of rope on wrong side*), work 1 more sc in same st, work 2 sc in each sc around — 20 sc.

Rnd 3: * Work 2 sc in next st — inc, 1 sc in next st; repeat from * around — 30 sc.

Rnd 4: * Work 1 sc in each of next 2 sts, 2 sc in next st; repeat from * around — 40 sc.

Rnd 5: * Work 2 sc in next st, 1 sc in each of next 3 sts; repeat from * around — 50 sc.

Continue in this manner, increasing 10 sc in each rnd, until circle is desired diameter. Do not inc directly over inc of previous rnd.

Next Rnd: Working in *back loop only,* work 1 sc in each st around. Remove marker.

Side: Working in *both loops* of all sts, work 1 sc in each st around and around until side is desired height plus 2 rows more for turn-over. Finish as follows: Cut rope leaving a 2″ end; without working over rope, sl st in next 3 sts. Fasten off. Turn top 2 rows to inside.

Cleaning

1. Wash in cold or lukewarm water, using mild soap. If badly soiled, scrub gently with soft-bristle scrub brush.

2. Rinse several times in cold or lukewarm water.

3. Shake off as much water as possible, then pat with turkish towel to remove excess moisture.

4. Let stand to dry, away from sun or heat.

110

Plant Hangers

Color Photograph, p. 110

For plant hanging, these macramé look-alikes take little time to make and inspire a variety of possibilities. Hang one alone or group several together. There are three different designs (fringed and unfringed), all crocheted with #15 cable cord, a hard, twisted, natural-colored twine available in 125-foot balls and usually sold as package cord. I found two brands at my local dime store, "Home-Ties" (January & Wood Co.) and "Gramco" (Wm. J. Graham Co.), but any similar weight cord will work.

The hanging cords are made with a heavier twine, about the same weight as drapery or Venetian blind pull-cords. This is also sold in dime stores, packaged in 45-foot skeins under the label "Home-Ties" and is referred to as Indoor Line. Two styles of hanging cords are shown (directions given after the plant hangers), but leather or suede thongs (sold in craft and leather supply stores) make an attractive alternative. The fringes and hanging cords are interchangeable.

Directions for the hangers are given to fit a standard clay pot 4¾ inches high. Size of hangers can be altered to fit larger or smaller pots by increasing or decreasing the length of the bands as indicated in the "Note" preceding directions for each hanger.

The clay pot is meant to be used only as a container to hold a smaller planted pot. To drip-proof the hanger pot, place a shallow glass or plastic saucer inside on the bottom — I used inexpensive round glass ashtrays. Set the potted plant in the hanger pot, filling the bottom with enough small pebbles to elevate the planted pot to about a half inch below the rim of the outer pot.

PLANT HANGER — UNFRINGED

MATERIALS (for each plant hanger):
1 ball #15 Cable Cord (125 ft.)
3 Plastic Rings — ⅝" outside diam.
Crochet Hook Size 0
Clay Pot — 4¾" high with 5¾" outside top diam. and 3¾" bottom diam.

NOTE: Before starting, divide the ball of cord into 4 equal balls. For larger hanger, use 2 balls of cord and divide each ball in half. Work tightly for best results. Use small crochet hook to weave in cord ends.

To lengthen or shorten hanger, increase or decrease the number of clusters in each side band. To change diameter of bottom, increase or decrease number of rows in each bottom band by multiples of 2.

First Ring Strip
Ring — Row 1 (Right Side): Holding cord at back of ring, yo hook, then insert hook through ring and under end of cord, yo and draw up a loop, yo and through both loops on hook — sc made, work 10 more sc over ring.
Row 2: Sl st in both loops of first sc and in next 8 sc.
First Band: Ch 1, do not turn, work 1 sc in next sc on ring, ch 1, turn, work first cluster: (insert hook in sc, yo and draw up a loop, yo and through first loop on hook) 3 times, yo and through all 4 loops on hook; * **Next Cluster:** Ch 1 to close cluster, ch 1 more, do not turn — wrong side, work a cluster in single loop at top of last cluster; repeat from * for total of 8 clusters, end with the 2 ch sts. *Do not cut cord;* place a safety pin in last st to hold.

Second Band: From right side insert hook in same sc as First Band, yo with new strand and draw up a loop, ch 1, work 1 sc in next sc on ring, ch 1, turn, work 8 clusters same as First Band, end with the 2 ch sts. Cut cord, pull cord out through last ch to hold. Attach paper tag with safety pin in ring to mark as First Ring Strip.

Second & Third Ring Strips: With 2 more rings, work 2 additional strips same as First Ring Strip. Mark accordingly; *do not remove markers until indicated.*

Join First Ring Strip to Second Ring Strip: From wrong side pick up dropped st of First Ring Strip, work 1 sc in top of cluster, from wrong side work 1 sc in top of fastened-off cluster of Second Ring Strip.

Bottom Band: * Ch 1, turn, work 1 sc in each of the 2 sc; repeat from * for total of 9 rows (including joining row) ending on wrong side. Fasten off.

Join Second Ring Strip to Third Ring Strip: From wrong side pick up dropped st of Second Ring Strip, join to Third Ring Strip same as before. Work Bottom Band the same.

Join Third Ring Strip to First Ring Strip: From wrong side pick up dropped st of Third Ring Strip; taking care not to twist bands, join to First Ring Strip same as before. Work Bottom Band the same. *Do not cut cord.* Remove markers.

Join Bottom Bands: * Taking care not to twist bands, from wrong side sl st in each sc at end of next Bottom Band toward left; repeat from * once, bring Third and First Bands together to form a circle, sl st in each sc of First Band bringing hook up through center hole. Fasten off.

Make any one of the hanging cords on p. 115.

PLANT HANGER WITH PLAIN FRINGE

MATERIALS (for each plant hanger):
1 ball #15 Cable Cord (125 ft.)
Several yards of Indoor Line for fringe (see Hanging Cords p. 115)
3 Plastic Rings — ⅝" outside diam.
Crochet Hook Size 0
Clay Pot — 4¾" high with 5¾" outside top diam. and 3¾" bottom diam.

NOTE: Before starting, divide ball of cord into 3 equal balls. For larger hanger, use 2 balls and divide 1 ball in half. Work tightly for best results. Use small crochet hook to weave in cord ends.

To lengthen or shorten hanger, increase or decrease the number of rows in each side band by multiples of 2. To change diameter of bottom, increase or decrease number of rows in each bottom band and each long band by multiples of 2.

First Ring Strip

Ring — Row 1 (Right Side): Holding cord at back of ring, yo hook, then insert hook through ring and under end of cord, yo and draw up a loop, yo and through both loops on hook — sc made, work 10 more sc over ring.

Row 2: Sl st in both loops of first sc and in next 7 sc.

First Short Band: Ch 1, do not turn, work 1 sc in next sc on ring, * turn, work 1 sc in *front loop* of sc; repeat from * for total of 18 rows (including first sc) ending on wrong side. Fasten off.

Long Band: From right side insert hook in same sc as last band, yo with new strand and draw up a loop, ch 1, work 1 sc in next sc on ring, continue same as First Short Band for total of 28 rows ending on wrong side. Fasten off.

Next Short Band: Work same as Long Band for total of 18 rows ending on wrong side. *Do not cut cord;* place a safety pin in last stitch to hold. Attach paper tag with another safety pin in ring to mark as First Ring Strip.

Second & Third Ring Strips: With 2 more rings, work 2 additional strips same as First Ring Strip. Mark accordingly; *do not remove markers until indicated.*

Join First & Second Ring Strips — Bottom Band

Row 1: From wrong side pick up dropped st of First Ring Strip, ch 1, turn, *working in both loops of all sts* work 1 sc in sc, from right side work 1 sc in end sc of fastened-off Short Band of Second Ring Strip.

Row 2: Ch 1, turn, 1 sc in each sc. Repeat Row 2 for total of 14 rows (including joining row) ending on wrong side. Fasten off.

Join Second & Third Ring Strips: From wrong side pick up dropped st of Second Ring Strip and join to fastened-off Short Band of Third Ring Strip same as before.

Join Third & First Ring Strips: From wrong side pick up dropped st of Third Ring Strip, *taking care not to twist bands* join to fastened-off Short Band of First Ring Strip the same as before. *Do not cut cord.* Remove markers.

Join All Bands: Continuing with last Bottom Band, ch 1, turn, 1 sc in each sc, * *taking care not to twist bands,* from right side work 1 sc in end sc of next Long Band, from right side work 1 sc in each sc of next Bottom Band; repeat from * around ending in last Long Band — 9 sc, join to form a circle by working 1 sc in first sc of first Bottom Band.

Bottom Cylinder: Work 1 sc in each sc around and around for 4 more rnds, do not join rnds, place a marker in first st of each rnd, end with sl st in next 3 sc. Fasten off.

Fringe: Combine 6 strands of Indoor Line (hanging cord) cut to desired length; tie center of strands together in a tight knot with a double strand of cable cord. Insert tying strand through bottom of Cylinder, pull up on strand from other end, drawing strands through Cylinder even with top edge. Knot tying strands to sts on wrong side of hanger. Untwist plies of fringe and trim evenly.

Make any one of the hanging cords on p. 115.

PLANT HANGER WITH BEADED FRINGE

MATERIALS (for each plant hanger):
2 balls #15 Cable Cord (125 ft.)
3 Plastic Rings — ⅝" outside diam.
Crochet Hook Size 0
Wood Barrel Beads — about 15 or 20
Clay Pot — 4¾" high with 5¾" outside top diam. and 3¾" bottom diam.

NOTE: Two balls have enough yardage for making a larger hanger if desired. Work tightly for best results. Use small crochet hook to weave in cord ends.

To lengthen or shorten hanger, increase or decrease the number of rows in each side band by multiples of 2. To change diameter of bottom, increase or decrease number of rows in each bottom band by multiples of 2.

First Ring Strip

Ring — Row 1 (Right Side): Holding cord at back of ring, yo hook, then insert hook through ring and under end of cord, yo and draw up a loop, yo and through both loops on hook — sc made, work 10 more sc over ring.

Row 2: Sl st in both loops of first sc and in next 8 sc.

First Band: Ch 1, do not turn, work 1 sc in next sc on ring, * turn, work 1 sc in *front loop* of sc; repeat from * for total of 23 sc (including first sc) ending on right side. Fasten off.

Second Band: From right side insert hook in same sc as First Band, yo with new strand and draw up a loop, ch 1, work 1 sc in next sc on ring, complete band same as First Band. *Do not cut cord.*

Bottom Band — Row 1: Ch 1, turn, working in *both loops,* work 1 sc in sc of same band, ch 1, *taking care not to twist bands* work 1 sc in end sc of First Band.

Row 2: Ch 1, turn, 1 sc in each st across — 3 sc. Repeat Row 2 five times ending on wrong side. Fasten off.

Second & Third Ring Strips: With 2 more rings, work 2 additional strips same as First Ring Strip. *Do not cut cord after completing last strip.*

Join Ring Strips: Continuing with Third Ring Strip, ch 1, turn, 1 sc in each sc across, (from right side work 1 sc in each sc across Bottom Band of next strip) twice — 9 sc, join to form a circle by working 1 sc in first sc of first bottom band.

Bottom Cylinder: Work 1 sc in each sc around and around for 4 more rnds, do not join rnds, place a marker in first st of each rnd, end with sl st in next 3 sc. Cut cord leaving a 3' strand.

First Fringe: Crochet remaining strand into a chain to within a few inches from end, pull end of cord out through last ch to hold.

Next Fringe: Cut an 8 strand and fold in half, from

right side insert hook in next sc of Cylinder, yo center of strand and draw up a loop; using one strand of cord, crochet strand into a chain as before; insert hook in *front loop* of same sc, yo with Second strand and draw up a loop, work chain as before. Work a fringe in each remaining sc of Cylinder same as last fringe — cut next strand in 10' length, then cut remaining strands in alternating lengths of 6, 8 and 10'.

Beads: Attach 1 or 2 beads to several chains at varying heights. To attach each bead: slide bead onto chain, tie chain over itself under bead to make a knot, slide bead down to meet knot. Untwist plies of cord at end of each fringe. Make any one of the following hanging cords.

HANGING CORDS

MATERIALS:

"Home-Ties" Indoor Line
  As a guide to quantity: 1 skein will make one
  Braided Cord about 40" long

Braided Cord

1. Mount hook or bracket from which the plant hanger will be suspended.
2. Decide on hanging level. Then measure between the hook or bracket and top of hanging rings of the plant hanger. This measurement is the hanging distance.
3. Cut 3 strands of cord in lengths four times this distance.
4. Hold the 3 strands together and fold in half. Make a knot by tying the end over itself about 1½" from fold, forming a loop at top end. Pull on each strand to remove slack and smooth out knot.
5. Secure loop to a stationary object and divide the 6 strands into 3 double strands. Plait as for a pigtail until braid (measuring from top of loop) equals about two-thirds the hanging distance.
6. Make second knot (same as first knot) at bottom of braid.
7. Measuring from top of loop, cut ends of the 6 strands so that total length of hanging cord is 1" more than hanging distance.
8. Divide the 6 strands into 3 double strands. Taking care not to twist strands, from wrong side insert ends of one double strand through one hanging ring. Make a knot at end of strands; trim excess fray. Attach other strands the same.

9. Pull up on hanging cord so that knots rest next to rings. Place plant hanger around clay pot and hang.

Plain Cord

1. Figure the hanging distance as in Steps 1 & 2 of Braided Cord.

2. Cut 3 strands of cord 2½ times this distance.

3. Repeat Step 4, then Steps 7–9 of Braided Cord.

Leather Thongs

1. Figure the hanging distance as in Steps 1 & 2 of Braided Cord.

2. Cut 3 thongs 1½ times this distance.

3. Tie the 3 thongs together at one end making a knot about 2″ from end. Pull on each thong to remove slack and smooth out knot. Leave short ends for fringe.

4. Measuring from *under* knot, cut thongs at other end so that strands are 1″ longer than hanging distance.

5. From wrong side insert end of one thong through one hanging ring; make a knot at end. Attach other 2 thongs the same.

6. Pull up on thongs so that knots rest next to rings. Place plant hanger around clay pot and hang.

Cleaning: Hangers can be hand-washed. If made with leather thongs, remove them before washing. Leave cotton hanging cords attached. See washing instructions on p. 142. Lay flat to dry. Let dry thoroughly before rehanging.

Daisy Tablecloth

Color Photograph, p. 111

The tablecloth we have come to know and feast upon is no longer just a culinary complement to buffets and soufflés. Somewhere between our coquilles Saint-Jacques and chocolate mousse it was whisked out from under us and landed smack in the middle of our living rooms.

Aside from the obvious splash of decorator dazzle, draped tablecloths are lifesavers for unaesthetic tables. Who will ever know about the spilled nail polish and water rings on this one?

The cloth is made of small hexagonal motifs sewn together into one giant hexagon that falls in scallops around the bottom. It's worked in Reynolds Parfait, a light acrylic yarn that has a nice draping quality. Directions are given for the size equivalent to a seventy-inch diameter circular fabric cloth, but you can make it any size by increasing or decreasing the number of rows. A shorter cloth can be draped over a full fabric one so it hangs halfway down for a layered look. Add fringe or tassels for a final flair.

The cloth will stretch one or two inches after hanging a few days; so keep this in mind when figuring on the finished length.

SIZE: Approx. 70″ across widest spread

MATERIALS:
  Reynolds Parfait:
    15 balls Gold #78
    13 balls Dk. Brown #42
  Alternates: Coats & Clark's Speed-Cro-Sheen Cotton or Lily Double Quick Crochet Cotton (if cotton thread is used, motif will measure approx. 4″ from point to point; thus fewer motifs will be required to make same size cloth)

Crochet Hook Size 1
Tapestry Needle #17

GAUGE: Each motif measures 3¾″ from point to point

NOTE: All rnds are worked from right side.

Motif (Make 271)
Rnd 1 — Center (Right Side): With Gold, ch 2, work 6 sc in 2nd ch from hook, join with sl st to first sc.

MOTIF DETAIL

118

Rnd 2 — Petals: * Ch 11, 1 dc in 4th ch from hook, 1 tr in next ch, 1 dtr (yo 3 times) in each of next 3 ch, 1 tr in next ch, 1 dc in next ch, 1 hdc in next ch, sl st in next sc of center; repeat from * 5 times, join with sl st to first sl st — 6 petals. Fasten off.

Rnd 3 — Border: Attach Dk. Brown in center ch at end of any petal, ch 3, work 4 dc in same ch, * ch 1, on same petal sk next 2 sts, 1 tr in next st, ch 1, sk next st, work 1 dtr in next st working off loops until 2 loops remain on hook, work 1 dtr in 4th ch (from center) of next petal working off loops until 3 loops remain on hook, yo and through all 3 loops — joint-dtr made, ch 1, sk next ch, 1 tr in next ch, ch 1, 5 dc in center ch at end of same petal; repeat from * 5 times ending last repeat with 2nd tr, ch 1, join with sl st to top of ch-3. Fasten off.

Assembly: With tapestry needle and Dk. Brown, sew motifs together following Arrangement Diagram for placement of first 3 rows. Continue joining motifs in this manner until there are 10 motifs across each of the 6 sides. Sew from right side with overcast stitch (see p. 143 for overcast stitch diagram), inserting needle through *back loop only* of each st and each ch. Start sewing in center st of one corner and end in center st of next corner. Work with an even tension to keep seam as elastic as motifs.

Blocking: With wrong side up, pin one section at a time to pressing board without stretching cloth. Block according to blocking instructions on p. 141.

Cleaning: Cloth can be hand-washed, but because of its size, dry cleaning is recommended. See p. 142 for dry cleaning information.

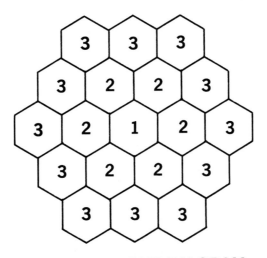

ARRANGEMENT DIAGRAM

Striped Place Mat with Coaster

Color Photograph, p. 122

Place mats are winning additions to dining décor whether you're serving two or twelve, and those you've made yourself are sure to add even more compliments to your culinary successes. The interlocking stitch pattern, worked in cotton thread, creates a woven texture that can be striped as shown or worked entirely in one color. The coasters are worked in a cluster pattern, carrying through the same colors of the mat. Together they make an attractive duo for outdoor dining or indoor brunches.

120

PLACE MAT

SIZE: Approx. 16″ × 12″ plus 2″ fringe

MATERIALS (for 2 mats):
  Coats & Clark's Speed-Cro-Sheen Cotton:
    3 balls each of Spanish Red and White
    2 balls Blue Sparkle
  Alternate: Lily Double Quick Crochet Cotton
  Crochet Hook Size 1

GAUGE: 6 sts = 1 inch
          2 rows = ¾ inch (measure along edge of rows)

Row 1 (Right Side): With Spanish Red, ch 98, work 1 dc in 4th ch from hook and in each ch across — 96 dc counting ch-3 as first dc.

Row 2: Turn, sl st in first dc, ch 2 — counts as first dc, 1 dc in each of next 2 sts, * ch 2, sk next 2 sts, 1 dc in each of next 2 sts; repeat from * across, end with 1 dc in each of last 3 sts working last dc in top of end ch (*Note: Always work last dc in top of end ch*). Fasten off.

Row 3: Turn, attach White in first dc as follows: holding thread at back of work, yo hook, then insert hook in st and under end of thread, yo and draw up a loop, yo and through both loops on hook — sc made, ch 2 — sc plus ch-2 count as first dc (*Note: When attaching a new strand, always work first dc in this manner*), 1 dc in each of next 2 dc, * holding ch-2 of previous row to *back* of work and taking care not to catch ch, work 1 dtr (yo 3 times) in each of next 2 sts on *2nd row below* — just under the ch-2, ch 2, sk next 2 sts; repeat from * across, end last repeat with 2 dtr, 1 dc in each of next 3 dc.

Row 4: Turn, sl st in first dc, ch 2, 1 dc in each of next 2 dc, ch 2, sk next 2 sts, * holding ch-2 of previous row *toward you,* work 1 dtr in each of next 2 sts on *2nd row below* — just under the ch-2, ch 2, sk next 2 sts; repeat from * across, end last repeat with 2 dtr, ch 2, sk next 2 sts, 1 dc in each of next 3 dc.

Row 5: Turn, sl st in first dc, ch 2, 1 dc in each of next 2 dc, * holding ch-2 of previous row to *back* of work, work 1 dtr in each of next 2 sts on *2nd row below* — just under the ch-2, ch 2, sk next 2 sts; repeat from * across, end last repeat with 2 dtr, 1 dc in each of next 3 dc. Fasten off.

Row 6: Turn, attach Spanish Red in first dc — first dc made, continue same as Row 4. Fasten off.

Row 7: Turn, attach Blue Sparkle in first dc — first dc made, continue same as Row 5. *Do not break thread.*

Rows 8 & 9: Continuing with Blue Sparkle, repeat Rows 4 & 5.

Row 10: Turn, attach Spanish Red in first dc — first dc made, continue same as Row 4. Fasten off.

Repeat Rows 3–10 for pattern, for total of 30 rows ending with Spanish Red row. *Do not break thread.*

Row 31: Ch 1, turn, sl st in each of first 3 sts, * holding ch-2 of previous row to *back* of work, work 1 dc in each of next 2 sts on *2nd row below,* sl st in each of next 2 sts; repeat from * across ending with sl st in each of last 3 sts. *Do not break thread.*

Edging: Ch 1, do not turn, 1 sc in last st, work in reverse sc as follows: * *working toward right,* ch 1, sk next st, insert hook in next st, *hook over yarn* and draw up a loop, yo and through both loops on hook — sc made; repeat from * across, end with 1 sc in each of last 2 sts. Fasten off.

Edging — Other Side: Working in single loop of foundation chain, from right side attach Spanish Red in base of ch-3, continue same as first side.

Fringe: (*Note: See p. 142 for instructions on knotting fringe.*) Wrap Spanish Red around a 3″ piece of cardboard. Cut thread at one edge. Combine 3 strands for 1 fringe; knot a fringe over dc at end of each row on short sides. Trim evenly.

Blocking: See p. 141 for blocking instructions.

Cleaning: See washing instructions on p. 142. Store mats flat.

COASTER

MATERIALS (for 2 coasters):
  Coats & Clark's Speed-Cro-Sheen Cotton:
    1 ball White
    25 ft. each of Blue Sparkle and Spanish Red
  Alternate: Lily Double Quick Crochet Cotton
  Crochet Hook Size 1
  Drinking Glass — at least 3½″ high with 3″ bottom diam.

NOTE: All rnds are worked from right side. Work tightly for best results. Coaster should fit snugly over glass, reaching no higher than 1″ from top rim.

Rnd 1 (Right Side): Starting at bottom, with White,

ch 1 loosely for center, ch 4 more, in center ch work (1 dc, ch 1) 11 times, join with sl st to 3rd ch at start — 12 dc and 12 spaces.

Rnd 2: Ch 5, 1 dc in next dc, * ch 2, 1 dc in next dc; repeat from * around ending with ch-2, join with sl st to 3rd ch at start.

Rnd 3: Ch 2, work first cluster: (yo, insert hook in same ch as join, yo and draw up a loop, yo and through 2 loops on hook) twice, yo and through all 3 loops on hook, * ch 5, work next cluster: yo, insert hook in next dc, yo and draw up a loop, yo and through 2 loops on hook, (yo, insert hook in same dc, yo and draw up a loop, yo and through 2 loops on hook) twice, yo and through all 4 loops on hook; repeat from * around, ch 3, join by working 1 dc in top of first cluster — 12 clusters and 12 loops.

Rnd 4: * Ch 5, 1 sc over center of next loop; repeat from * around, ch 3, join by working 1 dc in joining-dc of last rnd.

Rnd 5: * Ch 5, 1 sc over next loop; repeat from * around ending with ch-5, join with sl st to joining-dc of last rnd.

Rnd 6: Ch 2, complete first cluster in same st as join, ch 2, 1 sc over next loop, ch 2, * work cluster in next sc, ch 2, 1 sc over next loop, ch 2; repeat from * around, join with sl st to top of first cluster — 12 clusters.

Rnd 7: * Ch 5, 1 sc in top of next cluster; repeat from * around ending with ch-5, join with sl st to joining-sl st of last rnd — 12 loops.

Repeat Rnds 6 & 7 twice, then repeat Rnd 6 once.

Rnd 13: * Ch 3, 1 sc in top of next cluster; repeat from * around ending with ch-3, join with sl st to joining-sl st of last rnd.

Rnd 14: Ch 1, 1 sc in same st as join, work 3 sc over next ch-3 loop, * 1 sc in next sc, work 3 sc over next loop; repeat from * around, join with sl st to first sc. Fasten off.

Rnd 15: (*Note: See p. 141 for helpful hint on working over joinings.*) From right side attach Blue Sparkle in any sc as follows: holding thread at back of work, yo hook, then insert hook in st and under end of thread, yo and draw up a loop, yo and through both loops on hook — sc made, work 1 sc in each sc around, join with sl st to first sc. Fasten off.

Edging: Attach Spanish Red in any sc as before — sc made, work in reverse sc as follows: * *working toward the right,* insert hook in next st, *hook over yarn* and draw up a loop, yo and through both loops on hook; repeat from * around, join to first sc drawing thread through to wrong side. Fasten off. Stretch coaster over glass.

Cleaning: See p. 142 for washing instructions. Shape with fingers and stand up to dry, or place over glass and turn glass upside-down and let dry.

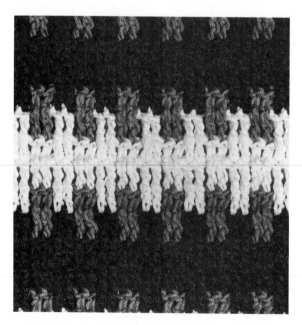

STITCH DETAIL

124

Round Place Mat

Color Photograph, p. 55

The once popular appeal of the so-called doily has long been lost to the new tastes of modern aesthetics, but as with anything else that falls from vogue, after enough time we're ready to take a second look.

Most doilies were made as antimacassars, but what used to be a fashionable furniture accessory now takes its place at the table. Much of the beauty of crochet is found in the intricate doily patterns, and this place mat design is an updated version of a traditional motif. It's reworked in a nubby acrylic yarn — a departure from the familiar white cotton that still captures the lacy look of the original.

As a point of interest, the term *antimacassar* — the protective covering placed on the backs and arms of upholstered furniture — is derived from Macassar oil (an export of Makassar, a city in Indonesia), which men used as a hair pomade long before the dry look.

125

BLOCKED SIZE: Approx. 16½″ in diameter

MATERIALS:
  Bucilla Paradise Banlon Yarn (1 oz. skeins):
    2 skeins of Med. Green for each mat
  Alternate: Coats & Clark's Speed-Cro-Sheen
    Cotton or Lily Double Quick Crochet Cotton
  Crochet Hook Size 1

GAUGE: 11 dc = 2 inches
    2 dc-rows = ¾ inch

NOTE: All rnds are worked from right side.

Rnd 1: Ch 1 loosely for center, ch 3 more — counts as first dc, work 15 dc in center ch, join with sl st to top of ch-3 — 16 dc.

Rnd 2: Ch 7, sk 1 dc, 1 dc in next dc, * ch 4, sk 1 dc, 1 dc in next dc; repeat from * 5 times, ch 4, join with sl st to 3rd ch at start — 8 dc and 8 spaces.

Rnd 3: Ch 3, 1 dc in first space next to ch-3, * ch 4, 1 dc in same space next to next dc, 1 dc in dc, 1 dc in next space next to same dc; repeat from * 6 times, ch 4, 1 dc in same space next to ch-3, join with sl st to top of ch-3 — 8 groups of 3-dc.

Rnd 4: Ch 3, 1 dc in next dc, 1 dc in first space next to same group, * ch 4, 1 dc in same space next to next group, 1 dc in each of next 3 dc, 1 dc in next space next to same group; repeat from * 6 times, ch 4, 1 dc in same space next to next group, 1 dc in next dc, join with sl st to top of ch-3 — 8 groups of 5-dc.

Rnd 5: Ch 3, 1 dc in each dc across first group, 1 dc in first space next to same group, * ch 3, 1 dc in same space next to next group, 1 dc in each dc across group, 1 dc in next space next to same group; repeat from * 6 times, ch 3, 1 dc in same space next to next group, 1 dc in each remaining dc of first group, join with sl st to top of ch-3.

Rnds 6–8: Repeat Rnd 5 three times — 8 groups of 13-dc at end of Rnd 8.

Rnd 9: Repeat Rnd 5 *except* work ch-5 between each group — 8 groups of 15-dc.

Rnd 10: Ch 3, 1 dc in each of next 5 dc, dec as follows: (yo, insert hook in next dc, yo and draw up a loop, yo and through 2 loops on hook) twice, yo and through all 3 loops on hook, * ch 5, 1 sc over center of ch-5 loop, ch 5, work dec over first 2 dc of next group, 1 dc in each of next 11 dc, work dec over last 2 dc of same group; repeat from * 6 times, ch 5, 1 sc over center of next loop, ch 5, work dec over first 2 dc of next group, 1 dc in each of next 5 dc, join with sl st to top of ch-3 — 8 groups of 13-dc with 2 loops between groups counting dec as 1 dc.

Rnd 11: Ch 3, 1 dc in each dc across first group to within 2 dc from end, work dec over last 2 dc, ** * ch 5, 1 sc over center of next loop * ; repeat from * to * across to next group, ch 5, work dec over first 2 dc of next group, 1 dc in each dc across group to within 2 dc from end, work dec over last 2 dc; repeat from ** 6 times; repeat from * to * across to next group, ch 5, work dec over first 2 dc of next group, 1 dc in each remaining dc of first group, join with sl st to top of ch-3.

Rnds 12–15: Repeat Rnd 11 four times — 8 groups of 3-dc with 7 loops between groups at end of Rnd 15.

Rnd 16: Ch 2, 1 dc in next dc, * (ch 5, 1 sc over next loop) 7 times, ch 5, dec as follows: (yo, insert hook in next dc, yo and draw up a loop, yo and through 2 loops on hook) 3 times, yo and through all 4 loops on hook; repeat from * 6 times, (ch 5, 1 sc over next loop) 7 times, join as follows: ch 5, yo and insert hook in next dc, yo and draw up a loop, yo and through 2 loops on hook, sk ch-2, insert hook in top of next dc, yo and draw up a loop pulling loop through both loops on hook.

Rnd 17: Sl st in each of first 3 ch of next loop, 1 sc over same loop, * ch 5, 1 sc over next loop; repeat from * around, ch 3, join by working 1 dc in first sc — 64 loops.

Rnd 18: * Ch 6, 1 sc over next loop; repeat from * around, ch 3, join by working 1 dc in top of joining-dc of last rnd.

Rnd 19: Repeat Rnd 18.

Rnd 20: * Ch 5, sl st in 3rd ch from hook — picot, ch 3, 1 sc over next loop; repeat from * around ending with ch-3, join with sl st to top of joining-dc of last rnd. Fasten off.

Blocking: The blocking and cleaning procedures may seem rather long and time-consuming, but don't let the preparation discourage you. A blocking pattern should be made to stretch stitches into a uniform smoothness. The extra touches really do make a difference and it's not as much trouble as it might appear.

1. Purchase enough white paper at an art supply store to cut a 20″ square for each mat. Brown or colored paper can stain fabric when damp. On one square (set the others aside until later) make a 16½″ diam. circle (the blocking circle should be ½″ larger than mat; finished size varies depending on materials used). Use a hard-lead pencil for drawing and press lightly; don't use ball-point or felt-

tip pens. To make circle: Mark dot at center of square, measure 8¼" (or half the diam. of the blocking circle) from center dot, marking dots at 1" intervals around; draw connecting lines between dots.

2. Mark pin placement: Making darker dots, divide circle into 4 equal parts as accurately as possible; then divide each quarter in half to make eighths; then each eighth in half to make sixteenths and so on until there are 64 marks.

3. Lay pattern on pressing board and insert a straight pin in each mark. With wrong side up, stretch one mat over the circle of pins, placing 1 picot-loop *over* each pin consecutively around. With moderately hot steam iron, steam close to fabric, *taking care not to let iron touch work.* Let dry thoroughly, then remove mat, *leaving pins in position.* Stretch rest of mats over pins, one at a time, and block the same. Save blocking pattern — this will be used as Master Pattern in cleaning instructions.

Cleaning: Mats can be dry-cleaned (see p. 142), but hand-washing is more practical. Before washing, you'll need 1 blocking pattern for each mat; all can be made in under 5 minutes.

1. Stack the remaining squares of paper on pressing board with Master Pattern from blocking instructions on top. Insert a pin in each corner to hold papers in place. Using a single pin, punch through all layers of paper at each pin mark. Pencil in a dot over pin marks on each new pattern.

2. Hand wash mats in cold water with mild soap — do not soak. Rinse thoroughly in cold water. Do not use starch. Roll in turkish towel and squeeze out excess water — do not wring.

3. Pin out on pressing board as in blocking instructions, 1 mat to a pattern. Let dry thoroughly, away from sun or heat. Store mats flat. Roll up patterns and save for future washings.

Beaded Wall Hanging

Color Photograph, p. 123

My fascination with macramé, frustratingly thwarted by lack of time, has produced little more than an envious perusal of everyone else's productivity. As a concession to the unkept promise that I will one day lay down the hook long enough to tackle some serious knots of my own, I have opted for innovation instead — a crocheted wall hanging utilizing the more interesting features of an actual macramé design.

It's worked in cotton thread, starting with a pair of rings, which can be of any material — wood, plastic, or metal — as long as they are close to the given measurements. The ring sizes can vary slightly, but the inside measurement between them should be 1½ inches.

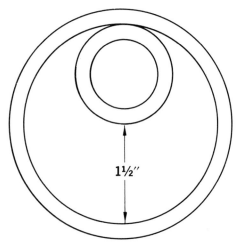

Your best source would be hardware and craft stores, jewelry counters (bracelets and earrings), and curtain accessory departments. If rings don't match in color or aren't particularly attractive, they can be covered with thread, as explained in the directions.

The beads on the bands and tassels are crocheted into the work as you go along and do not have to be prestrung. The rows of beads at the center of the middle and lower sections are sewn into spaces with a tapestry needle. The upper bands extending from the rings are joined to a wood dowel with a bead glued to each end.

SIZE: Approx. 7½″ × 30″

MATERIALS:
  Coats & Clark's Speed-Cro-Sheen Cotton:
    2 balls Canary Yellow
    1 ball Fudge Brown (optional) — for cover-
      ing rings
  Alternate: Lily Double Quick Crochet Cotton
  Crochet Hook Size 1
  Crochet Hook Size 7 (for attaching small beads
    only)
  Tapestry Needle #17
  Dark Brown Wood Beads:
    86 pieces 10 mm.
    30 pieces 14 mm.
  Large Ring — 3″ inside diam.
  Small Ring — 1″ inside diam.
  Wood Dowel — 3/16″ diam. (make points on
    each end with pencil sharpener for finished
    length of 7½″)
  White Craft Glue
  Brass Cup Hook for hanging

GAUGE: Approx. 6 sts = 1 inch
              (Work tightly for best results.)

**NOTE: Follow chart as a guide to sections. Hang-
ing is started at top end and worked to bottom end.
Left and right refer to hanging as viewed upside
down with front side facing.**

To Start — Cover Rings (Optional): For Large
Ring cut an 8 yd. length of Fudge Brown thread
and roll into a ball. Secure end of thread to ring
with a knot, then wind thread tightly around ring
until entire ring is covered. Knot the beginning
and end strands on one side of ring; cut thread ½″
from knot and glue ends down (wrong side). For
Small Ring, cut a 3 yd. length of Fudge Brown
thread and cover the same.

I — UPPER SECTION
A — Small Ring
*Note: If rings have been covered with thread,
work first row from right side around the half of
ring opposite knot.*
Row 1 — Right Side: Start with Size 1 Hook and
Small Ring. Holding thread at back of ring, yo
hook with Yellow, then insert hook through ring
and under end of thread, yo and draw up a loop,
yo and through both loops on hook — sc made,
work 14 more sc over ring — 15 sc.
Row 2: Ch 1, turn, work 1 sc in each sc across.
Row 3: Repeat Row 2. Fasten off.

Join Rings: With a piece of thread *temporarily* tie
the two rings together — the small inside the
large. For covered rings, place rings so that knots
are on wrong side at top end.

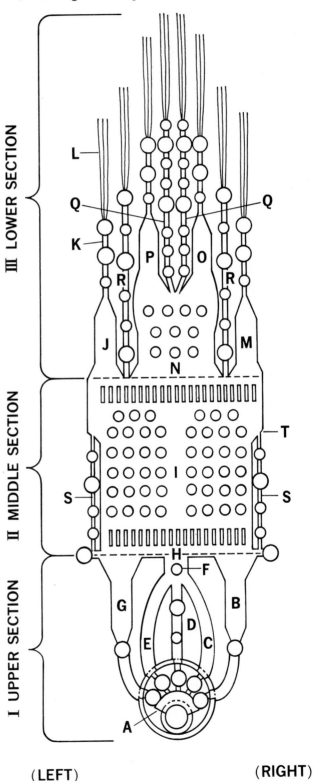

III LOWER SECTION

II MIDDLE SECTION

I UPPER SECTION

(LEFT)   (RIGHT)

DETAIL OF UPPER SECTION

B — First Band

Note: Hold rings with right side facing and with temporary join toward you.

Row 1: Attach new strand to section on Small Ring (A) as follows: holding thread at back of Large Ring, yo hook, then from *right side* insert hook in 2nd sc from end and under end of thread, yo and draw up a loop, yo and through both loops on hook — sc made (*Note: Attach all new strands in this manner*), attach Large Bead as follows — *Method # 1:* draw up loop on hook about 1″, remove hook, insert hook through bead hole, place loop over hook and draw through bead, pull on thread to remove slack from loop, ch 1 (*Note: Always work ch-1 after attaching each bead by this method*).

Row 2: Work over Large Ring as follows: draw up loop on hook to top of ring, ch 1, work 3 sc over Large Ring referring to diagram for position of stitches.

Row 3: Ch 1, turn, 1 sc in each of the 3 sc.

Rows 4–11: Repeat Row 3 eight times ending on wrong side.

Row 12: Ch 5, turn — counts as first dtr, attach Large Bead as follows — *Method # 2:* insert hook in next sc and draw up a 1″ loop, remove hook, insert hook through bead hole and draw 1″ loop through bead, remove hook, replace hook in dropped stitch, insert hook in loop at top of bead and pull on thread to remove slack from loop, yo and through both loops on hook, 1 dtr (yo 3 times) in last sc.

Row 13: Ch 1, turn, work 1 sc each in first dtr, center of bead loop, and top of ch-5.

Row 14: Ch 1, turn, 1 sc in each sc across.

Row 15: Ch 1, turn, 2 sc in first sc, 1 sc in next sc, 2 sc in last sc — 5 sc.

Row 16: Repeat Row 14 ending on right side.

Row 17: Ch 5, turn — counts as first dtr, 1 dtr in each sc across — 5 dtr.

Row 18: Ch 1, turn, 1 sc in each dtr working last sc in top of ch-5.

Rows 19 & 20: Repeat Rows 17 & 18.

Row 21: Ch 5, turn — counts as first dtr, 2 dtr in first sc, 1 dtr in each of next 3 sc, 3 dtr in last sc — 9 dtr.

Row 22: Repeat Row 18 ending on right side — 9 sc. Fasten off as follows: ch 1, cut thread, pull thread out through ch to hold; weave end through sts on wrong side (*Note: Always fasten off in this manner*).

C — Second Band

Row 1: From right side sk 2 sc from last band, keeping thread to wrong side of Large Ring attach new strand in next sc of Small Ring — sc made, attach Large Bead by Method # 1, work 2 more ch sts.

Row 2: Work over Large Ring as follows: draw up loop on hook to top of ring, ch 1, work 2 sc over ring referring to diagram for position of stitches.

Row 3: Ch 1, turn, 1 sc in each of the 2 sc.

Repeat Row 3 for a total of 24 sc-rows ending on right side. Fasten off.

D — Third Band

Row 1: Repeat Row 1 of Second Band (C).

Row 2: Work over Large Ring as follows: draw up loop on hook to top of ring, ch 1, work 1 sc over ring referring to diagram for position of stitches.

Row 3: Ch 1, turn, 1 sc in sc.

Rows 4–6: Repeat Row 3 three times ending on right side.

Row 7: Attach Small Bead by Method #1 (*Note: When attaching Small Bead, insert Size 7 Hook in bead hole to draw loop through, remove hook and pick up Size 1 Hook to continue*).

Row 8: Ch 1 more, 1 sc in 2nd ch from hook.

Row 9: Ch 1, turn, 1 sc in sc.

Row 10: Repeat Row 9 ending on right side.

Row 11: Attach Large Bead by Method #1.

Row 12: Repeat Row 8.

Repeat Row 9 four times ending on right side. Fasten off.

E — Fourth Band

Repeat Second Band (C). *Do not break thread.*

F — Join Second, Third, & Fourth Bands (C, D, & E)

Row 1: Ch 1, turn, work 1 sc in each of the 2 sc of Fourth Band (E); taking care not to twist bands, from wrong side work 1 sc in sc of Third Band (D) and 1 sc in each of the 2 sc of Second Band (C) — 5 sc.

Row 2: Ch 1, turn, 1 sc in each sc across.

Row 3: Repeat Row 2 ending on wrong side.

Row 4: Ch 3, turn — counts as first dc, 1 dc in next sc, attach Small Bead by Method # 2, 1 dc in each of next 2 sc.

Row 5: Ch 1, turn, work 1 sc each in first 2 dc, center of bead loop, next dc and top of ch-3 — 5 sc.

Row 6: Repeat Row 2 ending on right side. Fasten off.

G — Fifth Band

From right side sk 2 sc from Fourth Band (E) and attach new strand in next sc — sc made, work same as First Band (B). *Do not break thread.*

II — MIDDLE SECTION
H — Join Fifth, Center, & First Bands (G, F, & B) on Dowel

Note: Work each st in Row 1 over dowel.

Row 1: Continuing with Fifth Band (G), ch 1, turn — wrong side, place dowel so that turning ch is at front and thread is at back, draw up loop on hook to top of dowel, ch 1, work 1 sc in first sc as follows: insert hook in st and under dowel, yo and draw up loop through st and up to top of dowel, yo and through both loops on hook, work 1 sc in each sc across Fifth Band, work 1 sc over dowel only as follows: insert hook under dowel, yo hook and draw up loop to top of dowel, yo and through both loops on hook, work 7 more sc over dowel only, work 5 sc across Center Band, work 8 sc over dowel only, work 9 sc across First Band — 39 sc on dowel.

Row 2: Ch 1, turn, 1 sc in each sc across.

Row 3: Ch 5, turn (right side) — counts as first dtr, 1 dtr in each of next 2 sc, * ch 1, sk 1 sc, 1 dtr in next sc; repeat from * across ending with 1 dtr in each of last 3 sc.

Row 4: Ch 1, turn, work 1 sc in each dtr and each space across, work last sc in top of ch-5 — 39 sc.

Row 5: Ch 1, turn, 1 sc in each sc across.

Row 6: Repeat Row 5.

Row 7: Ch 4, turn — counts as first tr, 1 tr (yo twice) in each of next 2 sc, * (ch 2, sk 2 sc, 1 tr in each of next 2 sc) 4 times *, 1 tr in each of next 3 sc; repeat from * to * once, 1 tr in last sc.

Row 8: Ch 1, turn — right side, work 1 sc in each tr and 2 sc in each space across, work last sc in top of ch-4 — 39 sc.

Rows 9–16: Repeat Rows 7 & 8 four times.

Row 17: Ch 1, turn, work 2 sc in first sc, 1 sc in each sc across ending with 2 sc in last sc — 41 sc.

Row 18: Repeat Row 17 — 43 sc.

Row 19: Ch 4, turn — counts as first tr, 1 tr in each of next 6 sc, * (ch 2, sk 2 sc, 1 tr in each of next 2 sc) 3 times *, 1 tr in each of next 7 sc; repeat from * to * once, 1 tr in each of next 5 sc.

Row 20: Repeat Row 8 — 43 sc.

Row 21: Repeat Row 3.

Row 22: Repeat Row 4 — 43 sc. *Do not break thread.* Drop work temporarily and sew in beads. Attach a safety pin in last stitch to hold.

I — Beads

Sew Small Beads in ch-2 spaces of Middle Section as follows: Thread tapestry needle with same crochet thread; from right side, run thread through center of tr's at end of first row of spaces bringing needle out at first space, string a bead on thread and place in space; run thread through center of next group of sts to next space and string on a bead as before. Fill all ch-2 spaces with a bead in this manner.

III — LOWER SECTION
J — Left Panel

Row 1: Ch 1, turn, 1 sc in each of first 10 sc.

Row 2: Ch 1, turn, sk first sc, 1 sc in next sc — dec made, 1 sc in each sc across.

Rows 3–6: Repeat Row 2 four times ending on right side — 5 sc at end of Row 6.

Row 7: Ch 5, turn — counts as first dtr, 1 dtr in each of next 4 sc.

Row 8: Ch 1, turn, 1 sc in each dtr, work last sc in top of ch-5.

Row 9: Ch 5, turn — counts as first dtr, 1 dtr in next sc, ch 1, sk 1 sc, 1 dtr in each of last 2 sc.

Row 10: Ch 1, turn, work 1 sc in each dtr and ch-1 space, work last sc in top of ch-5.

Row 11: Ch 1, turn, sk first sc, 1 sc in next sc — dec made, 1 sc in each sc across.

Repeat Row 11 until 1 sc remains ending on right side.

K — Tassel

Note: Attach beads by Method # 1.

Ch 3, attach Small Bead, * (ch 4 more, attach Large Bead) twice, ch 1 more, 1 sc in 2nd ch from hook. Fasten off, leaving a 5″ strand.

L — Fringe

Cut four 9″ strands. From wrong side insert hook in last sc, fold strands in half, yo hook at fold and draw strands through sc to form a loop, draw ends and single 5″ strand through loop, pull on ends to tighten knot. Trim fringe to 2½″ from knot.

M — Right Panel

From *wrong side* attach new strand in 10th sc from end — sc made, 1 sc in each sc across — 10 sc. Complete same as Left Panel (J), starting with Row 2.

N — Center

Row 1: From *wrong side* sk 1 sc after Left Panel (J), attach new strand in next sc — sc made, 1 sc in next 20 sc leaving 1 sc free at end — 21 sc.

Row 2: Ch 1, turn, sk first sc, 1 sc in next sc — dec made, 1 sc in each sc across.

Rows 3–6: Repeat Row 2 four times ending on right side — 16 sc.

Row 7: Ch 4, turn — counts as first tr, 1 tr in each of next 2 sc, (ch 2, sk 2 sc, 1 tr in each of next 2 sc) 3 times, 1 tr in last sc.

Row 8: Ch 1, turn — right side, work 1 sc in each tr and 2 sc in each space across, work last sc in top of ch-4 — 16 sc.

Rows 9 & 10: Repeat Rows 7 & 8.

Row 11: Ch 1, turn, 2 sc in first sc, 1 sc in each sc across, end with 2 sc in last sc.

Row 12: Repeat Row 11 — 20 sc.

Row 13: Ch 4, turn — counts as first tr, 1 tr in each of next 2 sc, (ch 2, sk 2 sc, 1 tr in each of next 2 sc) 4 times, 1 tr in last sc.

Row 14: Repeat Row 8 — 20 sc.

Row 15: Ch 1, turn, 1 sc in each sc across. *Do not break thread.* Drop work temporarily and sew Small Beads in ch-2 spaces as before.

O — Right Center Panel

Row 1: Ch 1, turn — right side, 1 sc in first 9 sc.

Row 2: Ch 1, turn, sk first sc, 1 sc in next sc — dec made, 1 sc in each sc across.

Rows 3–5: Repeat Row 2 three times ending on right side — 5 sc.

Complete same as Left Panel (J), starting with Row 7; continue through K and L. *Trim fringe to 3½″.*

P — Left Center Panel

From *right side* sk 2 sc from Right Center Panel (O), attach new strand in next sc — sc made, 1 sc in next 8 sc — 9 sc. Complete same as Right Center Panel (O) starting with Row 2.

Q — Center Tassels

Note: Attach beads by Method # 1.

Between Left and Right Center Panels (P & O), attach new strand as follows: from *right side* insert hook in first sc and draw up a loop, ch 5, attach Small Bead; (ch 2 more, Small Bead) twice; ch 4 more, Large Bead; ch 4 more, Small Bead; ch 2 more, Small Bead; ch 2 more, Large Bead; ch 2 more, Small Bead; ch 1 more, 1 sc in 2nd ch from hook. Fasten off. Work fringe as before and trim to 3½″. Attach new strand in other sc and work 2nd Tassel the same.

R — Outer Tassels

Note: Attach beads by Method # 1.

Row 1: Between Center and Right Panel (N & M), from *right side* attach new strand in the free sc — sc made.

Row 2: Ch 1, turn, 1 sc in sc.

Rows 3–5: Repeat Row 2 three times ending on right side.

Row 6: Attach Large Bead.

Row 7: Ch 1 more, 1 sc in 2nd ch from hook.

Rows 8–11: Repeat Row 2 four times ending on right side.

Next Rows: (Attach Small Bead, work 5 rows of 1-sc) twice; Large Bead, 5 rows of 1-sc; Small Bead, 5 rows of 1-sc; Large Bead, ch 1 more, 1 sc in 2nd ch from hook. Fasten off. Work fringe as before and trim to 3½″. In the free sc at other side work 2nd Tassel the same.

S — Dowel Tassels

From right side, holding rings toward you, work 1 sc over right end of dowel as follows: holding thread at back of dowel, yo hook, then insert hook under dowel and under end of thread, yo and draw up a loop to top of dowel, yo and through both loops on hook, ch 2, attach Small Bead; ch 2 more, Small Bead; ch 4 more, Large Bead; ch 4 more, Small Bead; ch 6 more, join with sl st to end sc at T. At other side work 2nd Tassel the same.

Finishing: Glue Large Bead to each end of dowel.

Blocking: Place hanging right side up on pressing board, smooth out evenly and pin in place. Steam with moderately hot steam iron, *taking care not to let iron rest on fabric or touch beads.* Let dry thoroughly before removing. Remove temporary tie from rings and hang on hook as shown.

Cleaning: See p. 142 for washing instructions. Reglue dowel beads if they come off in washing.

Café Curtains

Color Photograph, p. 122

In the era of dark oak and brocade draperies, crocheted curtains used to hang in dreary gloom — hardly a compliment to their lovely handwork. With a little contemporary styling, though, those same curtains can take on a bright new look far removed from their dusty past. Their lacy eyelets now dapple the sunlight on my kitchen walls.

The curtains are worked in the knot stitch, a delicate pattern of loops and knots made with cotton thread. A simple shell edging completes each panel along with chain loops for hanging.

When planning the curtain size, the total width of the pair should be 1½ times the window width. The directions will accommodate any size.

133

MATERIALS:

Coats & Clark's White Speed-Cro-Sheen Cotton
As a guide to quantity: 7 balls will make the curtains shown, each panel of which measures 24″ wide × 18″ long
Alternate: Lily Double Quick Crochet Cotton
Crochet Hook Size 1

GAUGE: Measurement from center knot to center knot is 1 inch, horizontally or vertically

NOTE: Work tightly for best results.

Panel (Make 2)

Row 1 (Right Side): Starting at top edge, ch a multiple of 6 plus 2 more ch's for desired width, work 1 sc in 2nd ch from hook and in each ch across.

Row 2: Ch 1, turn, work 1 sc in first sc, work knot stitch as follows: * draw up loop on hook to measure ½″, yo and through loop on hook; with thumb, spread strands so that the loop is to the right side and the single strand is to the left side, insert hook between these 2 sections,

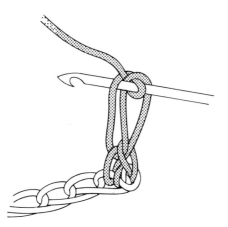

yo and draw up a loop, yo and through both loops on hook — first knot-stitch made; repeat from * once for 2nd knot-stitch — double-knot-stitch made, sk 5 sc, work 1 sc in next sc, ** work a double-knot-stitch, sk 5 sc, 1 sc in next sc; repeat from ** across.

Row 3: Work 3 knot-stitches, turn, working in first knot-stitch of previous row, work 1 sc between ½″ loop and single strand to right of center knot, then work 1 sc in corresponding space to left of *same* knot, * work a double-knot-stitch, 1 sc in each space to right and left of center knot of next knot-stitch; repeat from * across.

Repeat Row 3 for desired length ending on wrong side. Fasten off.

Edging

Rnd 1 — First Side: Holding work with foundation chain at top, from right side attach new strand in the *side* of last sc at left corner, 1 sc in same st, ch 2, working along edge of rows, work 1 sc in next single knot, * ch 2, 1 dc in next knot cluster, ch 2, 1 sc in next single knot; repeat from * across side ending with 1 dc in last knot cluster, work (ch 2, 1 dc) twice all in same knot — corner.

Lower Edge: Ch 2, 1 sc in next single knot, continue same as First Side, end with 1 dc in last knot cluster before single knot at corner, ch 2, work (1 dc, ch 2) twice and 1 dc all in next single knot — corner.

Second Side: Ch 2, 1 sc in next single knot, continue same as First Side, end with 1 sc in last single knot.

Top Edge (Hanging Loops): Working in single loops of foundation chain, sl st in first ch, ch 20, sl st in same ch, * sl st in each of next 6 ch, ch 20, sl st in same ch; repeat from * across, end with hanging loop in last ch. *Do not break thread.*

Rnd 2 (Edging): Continuing across First Side, work 1 sc in next sc, * ch 2, 1 dc in same st, sk ch-2, 1 sc in next st — shell made; repeat from * around 3 sides ending with 1 sc in last sc just before first hanging loop. Fasten off.

Blocking: See blocking instructions on p. 141.

Cleaning: Make note of measurements. Hand-wash according to washing instructions on p. 142. Pin out to original size to dry.

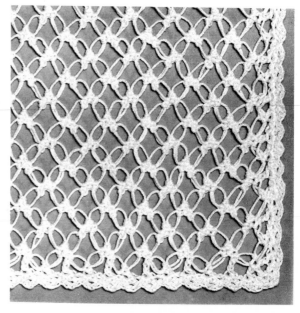

STITCH DETAIL

134

Carnation

Color Photograph, p. 123

Fresh flowers are always attractive decorating accents, but the cost of these fast-fading blooms usually limits our enjoyment to an occasional indulgence. I find the plastic and paper imitations aesthetically unsatisfactory and the beautiful silk flowers again can be quite expensive. So here's a crocheted carnation, almost the real thing — minus the aromatics.

I have a horticultural friend who proudly flaunts her ability to spot artificial plants and flowers from a distance at which the uneducated eye could not possibly make a distinction. However, this carnation has been part of my living room for several months and she still hasn't caught on.

It's improvised with parts of plastic flowers from the dime store. The blossom is formed by a ruffled circle crocheted with embroidery floss, which is slipped over a stem and gathered together at the bottom by a calyx (the green tubular part at the base of the flower). You may have to buy several flowers to get the necessary parts. Look for stems that have a small bulb on the flower end and a calyx that's about ½ inch in diameter and 1¼ inches long. Disassemble (they pull apart in pieces) and save the stems, calyxes, and appropriate leaves. Look specifically for carnations — the parts are usually botanically accurate.

A note on the calyx: If you have trouble finding a calyx the correct size, you can substitute a white tubular plastic knob (the type found on the end of Venetian blind and drapery cords) which can be painted green. The important thing is that the calyx fit tightly around the base of the crocheted circle to hold it up snugly in a tight cluster. If you use drapery knobs, make sure the stems you buy are thick enough to fill the hole at the bottom of the knob; otherwise, the blossom will wobble on the end of the stem.

The plastic stem allows you to combine the artificial flower with live complements. Make several carnations and arrange them in a spray with live greens or other flowers. Or try a *trompe l'oeil* twist by mixing the artificials with real carnations.

MATERIALS (for each flower):
  6 skeins of 6-strand Embroidery Floss — Deep Red
  Crochet Hook Size 1
  Tapestry Needle #19
  Stem and Calyx from plastic flower (leaves optional)

GAUGE: Finished circle is approx. 4″ in diam.

NOTE: All rnds are worked from right side.

Flower — Rnd 1 (Right Side): Ch 2, work 10 sc in 2nd ch from hook, join with sl st to first sc.
Note: Center hole should be small so circle will not slip past bulb at end of stem.
Rnd 2: Ch 3, 1 dc in same sc as join, * ch 2, 2 dc in next sc; repeat from * around, ch 2, join with sl st to top of ch-3 — 10 groups of 2-dc.
Rnd 3: Sl st in next dc and in next space, ch 3, work 1 dc, ch 2, 2 dc all in same space — first shell, * ch 2, work 2 dc, ch 2, 2 dc all in next space — next shell; repeat from * around, ch 2, join with sl st to top of ch-3 — 10 shells.
Rnd 4: Sl st in next dc and in next space, ch 4,

work 1 tr, ch 2, 2 tr all in same space — first shell, * ch 2, work 2 tr, ch 2, 2 tr all in next space — next shell; repeat from * around, ch 2, join with sl st to top of ch-4 — 20 shells.
Rnd 5: Ch 7, sl st in 3rd ch from hook — picot, 1 tr in next tr, ch 3, sl st in 3rd ch from hook — picot; continue around working 4 tr in each space and 1 tr in each tr with a picot between each st, end with picot, join with sl st to top of ch-4. Fasten off.

Assembly: Thread tapestry needle with a 15″ strand of embroidery thread, from right side weave thread through *base* of sts on Rnd 3, leave ends for tying. From right side insert bottom end of stem through center hole of crocheted circle and slide up to bulb end. Tie strands together drawing up sts into a tight cluster. Knot securely and cut off ends. Slide calyx on stem up over lower part of circle. Attach leaves if desired.

Cleaning: Remove blossom from stem and wash according to washing instructions on p. 142. Lay out flat to dry. Let dry thoroughly before reassembling.

APPENDIX

Terms and Abbreviations

ch — chain
dc — double crochet
dec — decrease
dtr — double treble

hdc — half double crochet
inc — increase
rnd — round
sc — single crochet
sk — skip

sl st — slip stitch
st(s) — stitch(es)
tr — treble crochet
yo — yarn over

An asterisk (*) or double asterisk (**) indicates that the instructions immediately following are to be repeated the given number of times in addition to the original.

Parentheses ( ): Whatever is enclosed in parentheses is worked the exact number of times stated *after* the parentheses.

The Basic Crochet Stitches

FOUNDATION CHAIN (ch)
Make a slip knot on hook about 6″ from end of

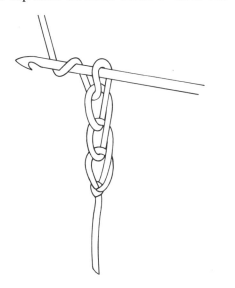

yarn. Pull end of yarn to tighten knot. Yarn over hook and draw through loop on hook — 1 chain made. Repeat for desired length. All of the following stitches are worked on a foundation chain.

SINGLE CROCHET (sc)
Insert hook into 2nd chain from hook — under the 2 upper strands: yarn over hook,

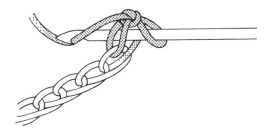

draw up a loop, yarn over hook,

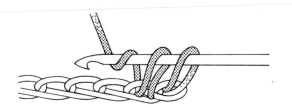

draw through both loops on hook, completing the stitch. Working in next stitch, repeat from beginning across to end.

HALF DOUBLE CROCHET (hdc)

Yarn over hook once, insert hook into 3rd chain — under the 2 upper strands, draw up a loop, yarn over hook,

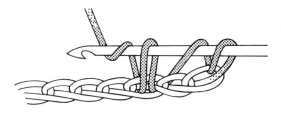

draw through all 3 loops on hook, completing the stitch. Working in next stitch, repeat from beginning across to end.

DOUBLE CROCHET (dc)

Yarn over hook once, insert hook into 4th chain — under the 2 upper strands, draw up a loop, yarn over hook, draw through first 2 loops on hook,

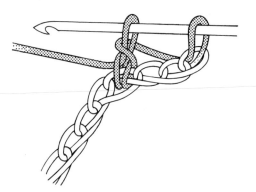

yarn over and through last 2 loops on hook, completing the stitch. Working in next stitch, repeat from beginning across to end.

TREBLE CROCHET (tr)

Yarn over hook twice, insert hook into 5th chain — under the 2 upper strands, draw up a loop,

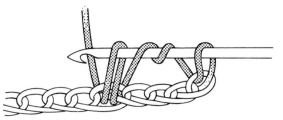

yarn over hook and through first 2 loops on hook,

yarn over hook and through next 2 loops, yarn over hook and through last 2 loops, completing the stitch. Working in next stitch, repeat from beginning across to end.

SLIP STITCH (sl st)

Make a foundation chain. Insert hook under the 2 upper strands of 2nd chain from hook, yarn over hook, with single motion draw through stitch and loop on hook. Repeat across to end.

Note: Always insert hook under the 2 upper strands of every stitch throughout work, unless otherwise specified in directions.

General Crocheting Information

STITCH GAUGE

The projects in this book are planned on the basis of working a specified number of stitches and rows to the inch. This is referred to as the *gauge*, which is given at the beginning of the instructions. It is important that the gauge is maintained; otherwise, the finished work will not be the correct size.

The size hook recommended will give the average worker the correct gauge. However, if you do not obtain the required gauge, change to another hook size to conform to the tension of your individual work. If your work is *too loose,* use a *smaller hook* to tighten the gauge. If your work is *too tight,* use a *larger hook* to loosen the gauge.

DYE LOTS

Color shades can vary between dye lots. When yarn is identified with a dye lot number, be sure to buy sufficient yarn of each color with the same number.

TAPESTRY NEEDLES

Tapestry needles are essential crocheting aids for weaving in yarn ends and sewing motifs and seams. The following is a suggested list of the most useful sizes, which are specifically mentioned in the instructions, but any needles of similar size will work as well. All should have blunt points.

#13 — for Bulky and Rug Weight Yarns

#17 — for Knitting Worsted, Medium-Weight Yarns, and Medium-Weight Cotton Threads

#19 — for Embroidery Floss, Pearl Cotton, and other Light-Weight Cotton Threads

MARKERS

Safety pins make ideal markers.

CROCHETING OVER JOININGS (for use when crocheting in rounds all worked from the right side):

When crocheting a round with a new strand of yarn, work over the *joining* of previous round as follows: Work under both loops of the *joining sl st* instead of in the stitch where the sl st is worked; sk the stitch where join is made and work next stitch in following stitch. This eliminates the open area between stitches and makes the joining of each round invisible.

Blocking Instructions

With wrong side up, pin item on pressing board to given measurements. Steam lightly with moderately hot iron over a wet cloth, taking care not to let weight of iron rest upon any one spot. Allow to dry thoroughly before removing from board.

If item is fringed, steam fringe in the same manner and, while damp, comb with fingers to smooth out strands.

Helpful Hints: Use plastic-tipped straight pins; they're rust-proof and easy on the fingers. Corrugated pattern-cutting boards, available in sewing notions stores, make ideal pressing boards. The grid surface, marked in 1″ intervals, saves measuring time and provides preset straight lines. Pins are easily inserted and, so far, my board has not reacted unfavorably to the moisture and heat from steaming. It folds up for easy storage and opens out flat, providing a fairly large work area which will accommodate most items. Large pieces, such as afghans and bedspreads, can be blocked in sections.

Hand-Washing Instructions

1. Wash in cold or lukewarm water, using mild soap or Woolite.
2. Rinse several times in cold or lukewarm water until every trace of soap is removed. Last rinse water should be clear.
3. Squeeze out excess water — do not twist or wring. Roll in turkish towel and squeeze again.
4. Remove from towel at once. Lay out on pressing board and shape to original measurements. Pin in place.
5. Let dry, away from sun or heat. Allow to dry *thoroughly* before removing.

Note: Never allow crocheted articles to soak for any long period of time; never use hot water, strong soap, or detergent; never hang to dry.

Dry Cleaning

When having an item dry-cleaned, use a reliable cleaner who specializes in handwork. Give cleaner original measurements so that item can be blocked to proper size.

How to Make a Fringe

1. Wind yarn around a piece of cardboard cut to the width indicated in directions. Cut yarn at one edge.

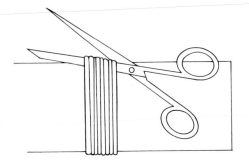

2. Place work right side up with edge to be fringed toward you.

3. Combine the specified number of strands for 1 fringe. Fold strands in half.
4. From wrong side, insert hook in space or stitch where fringe is desired. Bring center fold of strands through, forming a loop.

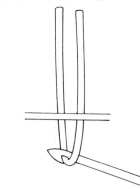

5. Leaving hook in loop, use hook to gather up strands and draw through loop.

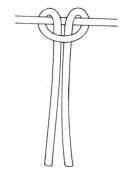

6. Pull ends to tighten into knot. Trim evenly.

How to Make a Fail-Safe Tassel

1. Cut a piece of cardboard the width specified in directions.
2. Lay a 12″ strand of yarn lengthwise across cardboard. Wind another length of yarn crosswise

142

around cardboard and over strand the number of times specified.

3. Slip loops off cardboard.

4. Tie loops together with the 12″ strand. To make a secure knot, wrap one end *twice* over the other and draw up tight. Tie again wrapping one end once over the other. Cut loops at opposite end.

5. For an easier and neater tassel, slide a plastic or metal ring over tying ends and down over head of yarn about ½″ to 1″ from top depending on size of tassel. Ring should fit as tightly as possible.

6. Cut another strand about 15″ long and wrap one end several times around yarn just above ring. Thread end of wrapping strand through tapestry needle and draw through center of tassel — do not tie a knot.

7. Trim yarn ends evenly and remove ring.

8. To smooth out ''wrinkles'' in yarn, steam with steam iron or hold over the spout of a boiling tea kettle.

9. Use tying strands to attach tassel unless otherwise specified.

Overcast Stitch for Sewing

In this book the overcast stitch is used for sewing together all crocheted pieces. The following diagram shows sewing in the *back loop:* the needle

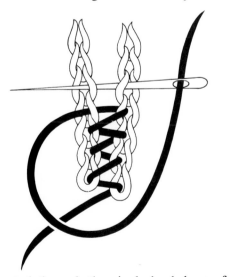

is inserted through the single back loop of each stitch on both pieces — 2 loops on needle. Some directions will call for sewing in *both loops,* where the needle is inserted through both the front and back loop of each stitch on both pieces — 4 loops on needle.

Pillow Forms

There are two basic types of pillows: the box-edge, which has dimensional sides, and the knife-edge — the pillow tapers from its center fullness to a sharp edge. All the pillow designs in this book are knife-edge. Premade muslin forms and molded foam forms are generally available in squares from 10″ to 16″ and can be used when the pillow cover is a standard size square, but you will need to make your own in most cases.

Pillow forms are really quite simple to make. Use a good-quality unbleached muslin for the casing. Finished, unstuffed casing should be 1″ longer and 1″ wider than crocheted pillow cover — form should be a little larger than cover for a snug fit. Directions for each pillow specify the correct cutting size, allowing for seams and the extra length and width.

There are a number of fillers one can use for stuffing, and having experimented with a few, I'll pass along my experience.

Foam chips are springy and light and give pillows good resiliency, if you can get them inside the casing. I never can. Most of them either bounce off into the hidden recesses of my apartment (to be found weeks later when sweeping under the sofa) or mysteriously attach themselves to the walls and hang in supernatural suspension waiting to be picked off one by one. This same magnetic quality also makes a tortuous job of retrieving them from the rugs.

Down, the soft, fluffy feathers from geese, ducks, and other water birds, is luxuriously soft and long-wearing, but in addition to the allergy problem it presents for some people, it's also luxuriously expensive.

Kapok is a silky, cottony fiber that clings and crawls over anything it touches, leaving something resembling a snail trail. Aside from its slithery instincts, it mats and tends to become lumpy and lifeless.

Then I found polyester fiber filling. It looks like surgical cotton and usually comes in 1 lb. bags. It doesn't cling, creep, crawl, or fly, and stays quietly plump inside all my pillows. Dime stores carry it and I've also seen it for sale in the bedding section of department stores. Any reference to filling or stuffing is calculated on the assumption that this is what you're going to use.

TO MAKE PILLOW FORM
Materials:
  Muslin
  Polyester Fiber Filling

1. Fold muslin to make double thickness. With a pencil and ruler draw pillow dimensions on muslin as specified in directions, making sure corner angles are straight. Cut out through both thicknesses.

2. Sew pieces together ½″ from edge leaving a 6″ to 10″ opening at center of one side for stuffing — the larger the form, the larger the opening. Reinforce with another row of stitching over first row. Clip diagonally across corners.

3. Press back each seam allowance of opening to wrong side.

4. Turn to right side and push out corners. Stuff with filling. As a guide, use about ¾ to 1 lb. of polyester filler per square foot — the larger the pillow, the more stuffing per square foot. (Other fillers have varying proportions.)

5. With needle and thread sew opening closed with overcast stitch.

6. Beat pillow with hands to distribute stuffing evenly.

How to Work Jacquard Crochet

Jacquard is a term that refers to changing off colors as you work to form a design or picture in the crocheted fabric. It's one of the most useful techniques in crochet and probably the least understood. I have yet to find a satisfactory explanation on how to work jacquard crochet, and since many of the projects in this book incorporate the technique, detailed instructions follow.

Jacquard patterns are made in either double crochet or single crochet stitches. The design is worked from a chart of squares with symbols or shadings used to designate the yarn colors. Once you understand the procedure of changing and adding colors, the chart is all that's necessary to work the design. Naturally the advantages of working directly from a chart are to eliminate lengthy instructions and to simplify the mechanics.

The squares on the chart represent the stitches, which are counted as you work. When working in double crochet, one square = 2 dc; when working in single crochet, one square = 1 sc. The chart is read from the bottom to the top. On right-side rows, you read the chart from right to left (←); on wrong-side rows, you read left to right (→). The first row of the design can start on either the right side or wrong side of work. An arrow is used to indicate direction of first design row.

Color changes are made in three ways: by attaching a new strand of yarn, by picking up a strand from previous row that has been dropped to wrong side, or by picking up a strand that has been carried along current row. Some people carry most of the colors but I prefer to carry yarn only when the color to be carried matches the color of row it is carried over; otherwise, the carried yarn shows through between the stitches on the right side. For the same reason, do not crochet over yarn ends as you work; weave in ends separately with tapestry needle just along surface of the same color stitches on wrong side.

I like to work jacquard patterns with a tight gauge. The work is smoother and the design has more definition. Tight work is particularly necessary when making wall hangings. If stitches are loose, the hanging will sag, pulling the design out of shape. Because of the disproportionate ratio between the stitch and row gauge, the crocheted design tends to be more compressed than the charted design. This compression is more evident with single crochet jacquard than with double crochet, but does not detract from the finished piece.

When working an intricate pattern in which there are continuous color changes, you will have many strands of yarn hanging from the back of your work. There are various methods for handling the yarn and the following suggestions and pointers are offered only as helpful information. There is no one best method; how you work is simply a matter of personal preference.

I prefer to work with long lengths of yarn, dividing a skein of each color in thirds or fourths and rolling each into a ball. As each strand is discontinued from use, it is cut off and pulled free from the rest of the yarn and set aside until needed again. Working with long strands eliminates excessive yarn waste; the yarn is cut after the necessary amount has been used, rather than precutting each strand and creating a build-up of scraps, many of which are too short to reuse. The biggest drawback to this method is the mess. As you change colors, the strands twist around each other, forming loose tangles, and you have to stop after every third or fourth row and untwist.

A lot of people just can't work with all that confusion hanging from the back. If you prefer to work in a more organized atmosphere, strands can be wrapped around bobbins or tied in butterfly knots, a commonly used macramé method. Bobbins, usually made of plastic and used for knitting and crochet alike, come in various sizes for different yarn weights. Match the size to the yarn and wind as full as possible. Butterfly knots are formed by wrapping the yarn into small bundles in a manner which allows the yarn to slide out as it's needed. Cut yarn in lengths of about 5' or 6', or as long as possible without making the knot overly bulky. After attaching one end of strand to work, tie as follows:

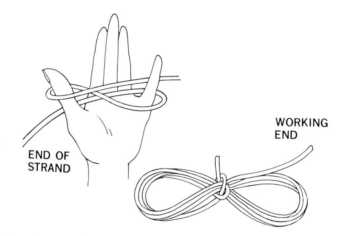

END OF
STRAND

WORKING
END

Wrap yarn around thumb and little finger in a figure eight motion, beginning the wind a convenient length from where the strand is attached. Do not wind from the bottom end, because yarn will not slide out. Self-tie around the center with last few inches of yarn or secure with a rubber band. When using bobbins or butterfly knots, keep yarn wound close to work, releasing enough of each color as needed.

Personally, I find bobbins and knots time-consuming and annoying. I get too bogged down fussing with the yarn while trying to count stitches and make color changes, and the constant distraction hampers my efficiency. But what's good for one won't necessarily work for another, and as you gain more experience with jacquard patterns you will develop the best method to suit your individual work habits.

Directions are given for making a practice swatch for both the double and single crochet techniques. The same chart is used for both methods. The instructions are just a guide; color changes vary with each pattern and knowing how to anticipate color changes and where and when to carry colors will come with practice. The total objective is to reproduce the charted design in the crocheted fabric as neatly and evenly as possible.

MATERIALS:

4-ply Knitting Worsted:
  1 oz. each of White (W), Green (G), and
    Orange (O)
Crochet Hook Size G
Tapestry Needle #17

NOTE: Instructions refer to colors by letter. Keep yarn ends and dropped colors on wrong side of work. Refer to chart as you work.

DOUBLE CROCHET JACQUARD TECHNIQUE — PRACTICE SWATCH

GAUGE: 4 dc = 1 inch
2 rows = ⅞ inch

NOTE: Each square on chart = 2 dc.

Row 1 (Right Side): With W, ch 24, work 1 dc in 4th ch from hook and in each ch across — 22 dc counting beginning ch as first dc.

Row 2: Turn — wrong side, sl st in first dc, ch 2 (*Note: Turning ch is worked in this manner to maintain an even edge — turning ch always counts as first dc*), work 1 dc in each st across working last dc in top of end ch (*Note: Always end row with 1 dc in top of end ch*).

Row 3: Turn — right side, work turning ch, 1 dc in each of next 8 sts, yo and insert hook in next st, yo and draw up a loop, yo and through 2 loops on hook, yo with G leaving a 6″ strand on wrong side, draw G through both loops on hook (*Note: When attaching a new strand, always leave a 6″ end on*

wrong side), pull on W to remove slack and drop to wrong side (*Note: After changing to next color, always pull gently on first color to remove slack*); with G work 1 dc in each of next 2 sts completing last dc with a new strand of W, remove G slack, cut G leaving a 6″ strand on wrong side (*Note: When cutting off a color, always leave 6″ end on wrong side*); with W work 1 dc in each of next 10 sts.

Row 4: Turn — wrong side, work turning ch, 1 dc in each of next 7 sts completing last dc with a new strand of G, drop G and W to wrong side; with G work 1 dc in each of next 4 sts, pick up W from last row and hold along edge of work, continuing with G work 1 dc in each of next 2 sts crocheting over W, work last G dc until 2 loops remain on hook, pull on carried W to remove slack (*Note: Always pull gently on any carried yarn before proceeding with that color*), yo with W and draw through both loops on hook, cut G and drop to wrong side; with W work 1 dc in each of next 8 sts.

Row 5: Turn — right side, work turning ch, 1 dc in each of next 5 sts completing last dc with a new strand of G, drop W; with G work 1 dc in each of next 4 sts completing last dc with O, drop G; with O work 1 dc in each of next 2 sts completing last dc with a new strand of G, cut O; with G work 1 dc in each of next 2 sts, pick up W from last row and hold along edge of work, continuing with G work 1 dc in each of next 2 sts crocheting over W, complete last G dc with carried W, cut G; with W work 1 dc in each of next 6 sts.

Row 6: Turn — wrong side, work turning ch, 1 dc

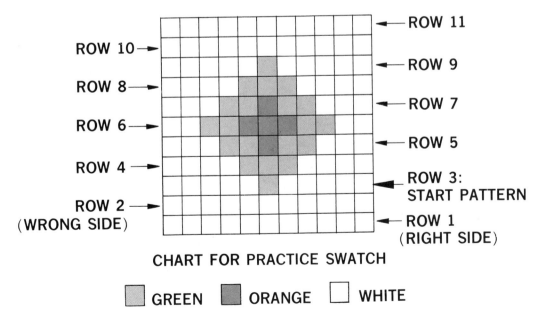

CHART FOR PRACTICE SWATCH

■ GREEN ■ ORANGE □ WHITE

in each of next 3 sts completing last dc with a new strand of G, cut W; with G work 1 dc in each of next 4 sts completing last dc with a new strand of O, cut G; with O work 1 dc in each of next 6 sts carrying G over last 2 sts, complete last O dc with carried G, drop O; with G work 1 dc in each of next 4 sts carrying W over last 2 sts, complete last G dc with carried W, drop G; with W work 1 dc in each of next 4 sts.

Row 7: Turn — right side, work turning ch, 1 dc in each of next 5 sts carrying G over last 2 dc, complete last W dc with carried G, cut W; with G work 1 dc in each of next 4 sts carrying O over last 2 dc, complete last G dc with carried O, cut G; with O work 1 dc in each of next 2 sts completing last dc with a new strand of G, cut O; with G work 1 dc in each of next 4 sts completing last dc with a new strand of W, drop G; with W work 1 dc in each of next 6 sts.

Row 8: Turn — wrong side, work turning ch, 1 dc in each of next 7 sts carrying G over last 2 dc, complete last W dc with carried G, cut W; with G work 1 dc in each of next 6 sts completing last dc with a new strand of W, drop G; with W work 1 dc in each of next 8 sts.

Row 9: Turn — right side, work turning ch, 1 dc in each of next 9 sts carrying G over last 2 dc, complete last W dc with carried G, cut W; with G work 1 dc in each of next 2 sts completing last dc with a new strand of W, cut G; with W work 1 dc in each of next 10 sts.

Row 10: Turn, work turning ch, with W work 1 dc in each st across.

Row 11: Repeat Row 10. Fasten off. Weave in ends with tapestry needle.

SINGLE CROCHET JACQUARD TECHNIQUE — PRACTICE SWATCH

GAUGE: 9 sc = 2 inches
5 rows = 1 inch

NOTE: Each square on chart = 1 sc.

Row 1 (Right Side): With W, ch 12, work 1 sc in 2nd ch from hook and in each ch across — 11 sc.

Row 2: Ch 1, turn — wrong side, work 1 sc in each sc across.

Row 3: Ch 1, turn — right side, 1 sc in each of first 4 sts, insert hook in next st and draw up a loop, yo with G leaving a 6″ strand on wrong side, draw G through both loops on hook (*Note: When attaching a new strand, always leave 6″ end on wrong side*), pull on W to remove slack and drop to wrong side (*Note: After changing to next color, always pull gently on first color to remove slack*); with G draw up a loop in next st, drop G to wrong side, yo with a new strand of W and draw through both loops on hook, remove G slack; with W work 1 sc in each of next 5 sts.

Row 4: Ch 1, turn — wrong side, 1 sc in each of

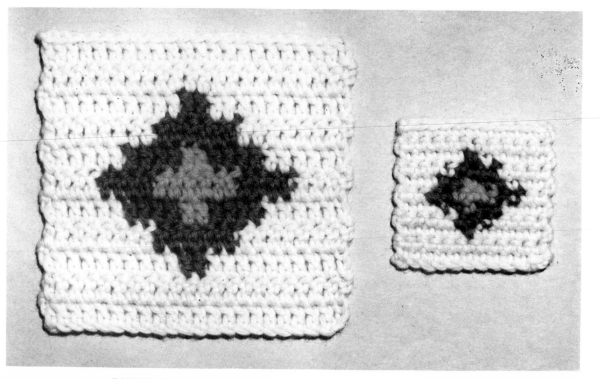

DOUBLE CROCHET SWATCH   **SINGLE CROCHET SWATCH**

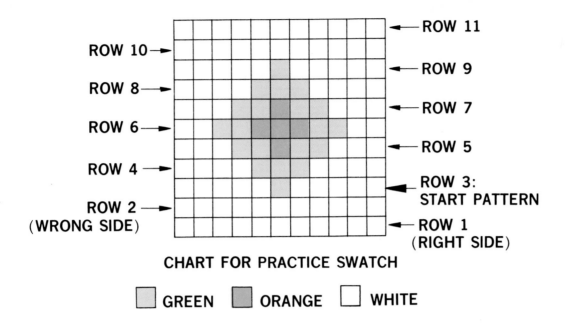

CHART FOR PRACTICE SWATCH

☐ GREEN ■ ORANGE ☐ WHITE

first 3 sts, draw up a loop in next st, drop W to wrong side next to the last st made, pick up G from last row, yo and draw through both loops on hook; with G work 1 sc in next st working over crossed G yarn (*Note: Where yarn crosses a st, always work over crossed yarn when working in that st; never cross yarn back more than 1 st – if more sts, attach new strand*), 1 sc in next st, pick up W from last row and hold along edge of work, with G draw up a loop in next st working over W, complete st with W, drop G to wrong side; with W work 1 sc in each of next 4 sts.

Row 5: Ch 1, turn — right side, 1 sc in each of first 2 sts, draw up a loop in next st, drop W to wrong side, complete st with G from last row; with G work 1 sc in next st working over crossed G yarn, draw up a loop in next st, yo with O and complete st, drop G to wrong side; with O draw up a loop in next st, complete st with a new strand of G, drop O to wrong side; with G work 1 sc in next st, pick up W from last row and hold along edge of work, with G draw up a loop in next st working over W, drop G to wrong side, complete st with W; with W work 1 sc in each of next 3 sts.

Row 6: Ch 1, turn — wrong side, 1 sc in first st, draw up a loop in next st, drop W to wrong side, complete st with G; with G work 1 sc in next st, draw up a loop in next st, drop G to wrong side, complete st with O; with O work 1 sc in each of next 2 sts, holding G along edge of work draw up a loop in next st, complete st with G, drop O to wrong side; with G work 1 sc in next sc, holding W

along edge of work draw up a loop in next st, complete st with W, drop G to wrong side; with W work 1 sc in each of next 2 sts.

Row 7: Ch 1, turn — right side, 1 sc in each of first 2 sts, holding G along edge of work draw up a loop in next st, drop W to wrong side, complete st with G; with G work 1 sc in next st, holding O along edge of work draw up a loop in next st, complete st with O, cut G leaving a 6″ strand and drop to wrong side (*Note: When cutting off a color, always leave a 6″ end on wrong side*); with O draw up a loop in next st, drop O to wrong side, complete st with G, cut O; with G work 1 sc in next st, draw up a loop in next st, drop G to wrong side, complete st with W; with W work 1 sc in each of next 3 sts.

Row 8: Ch 1, turn — wrong side, 1 sc in each of first 3 sts, holding G along edge of work draw up a loop in next st, complete st with G, drop W to wrong side; with G work 1 sc in each of next 2 sts, draw up a loop in next st, drop G to wrong side, complete st with W; with W work 1 sc in each of next 4 sts.

Row 9: Ch 1, turn — right side, 1 sc in each of first 4 sts, holding G along edge of work draw up a loop in next st, drop W to wrong side, complete st with G, cut W; with G draw up a loop in next st, drop G to wrong side, complete st with W, cut G; with W work 1 sc in each of next 5 sts.

Row 10: Ch 1, turn, 1 sc in each st across.

Row 11: Repeat Row 10. Fasten off. Weave in ends with tapestry needle.

149

How to Work Filet Crochet

This is a type of crochet that consists of blocks and spaces arranged to form a pattern or picture and is also worked from a chart of squares. The shaded squares represent blocks and the open squares (referred to as the mesh) represent spaces. The double crochet stitch is used throughout.

In a group of blocks, 4 double crochets make the first block and 3 double crochets make each additional block in the same group. For instance, 2 blocks require 7 dc, or 3 blocks require 10 dc. The mesh is formed by working 2 ch sts between each dc.

As with jacquard patterns, the chart is read from the bottom to the top. On right-side rows, you read the chart from right to left (←); on wrong-side rows, you read left to right (→). The first row of the design can start on either the right side or wrong side of work. An arrow is used to indicate direction of first design row.

I also prefer to work filet crochet with a tight gauge. Tight work produces sharper contrast between the design and the background mesh. But make sure that the squares in the crocheted work measure the same, both horizontally and vertically, to keep the design even.

Both filet projects included in the book are worked with Coats & Clark's Knit-Cro-Sheen cotton. Directions for making the practice swatch are given using this thread.

FILET CROCHET — PRACTICE SWATCH

MATERIALS:
Coats & Clark's Knit-Cro-Sheen Cotton
Crochet Hook Size 9

GAUGE: 4 horizontal or vertical squares = 1″ (When counting squares for gauge: for each horizontal square, count 1 dc plus following space; for each vertical square, count chain plus following space.)

NOTE: Refer to chart as you work.

Row 1 (Right Side): Ch 44, work 1 dc in 8th ch from hook, * ch 2, sk 2 ch, 1 dc in next ch; repeat from * across — 13 spaces made.

Row 2: Ch 5, turn — wrong side, sk first space, 1 dc in next dc, * ch 2, 1 dc in next dc; repeat from * across working last dc in 3rd ch at end.

Row 3: Ch 5, turn — right side, sk first space, 1 dc in next dc, (ch 2, 1 dc in next dc) 5 times — 6 spaces made, 2 dc in next space, 1 dc in next dc — 1 block made, (ch 2, 1 dc in next dc) 5 times, ch 2, 1 dc in 3rd ch at end — 6 spaces made.

Row 4: Ch 5, turn — wrong side, sk first space, 1 dc in next dc, (ch 2, 1 dc in next dc) 4 times — 5 spaces made, 2 dc in next space, 1 dc in each of

150

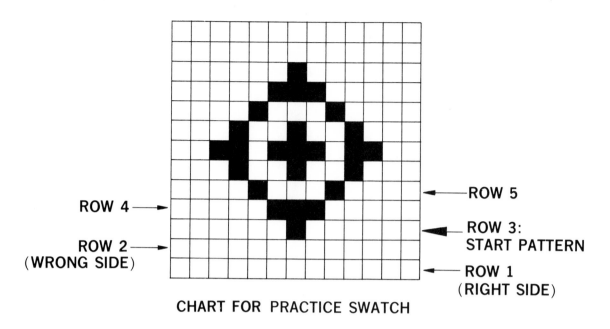

CHART FOR PRACTICE SWATCH

next 4 dc, 2 dc in next space, 1 dc in next dc — 3 blocks made, (ch 2, 1 dc in next dc) 4 times, ch 2, 1 dc in 3rd ch at end — 5 spaces made.

Row 5: Ch 5, turn — right side, sk first space, 1 dc in next dc, (ch 2, 1 dc in next dc) 3 times — 4 spaces made, 2 dc in next space, 1 dc in next dc — 1 block made, (ch 2, sk 2 dc, 1 dc in next dc) 3

times — 3 spaces made, 2 dc in next space, 1 dc in next dc — 1 block made, (ch 2, 1 dc in next dc) 3 times, ch 2, 1 dc in 3rd ch at end — 4 spaces made.

Continue in this manner following chart for remainder of work.

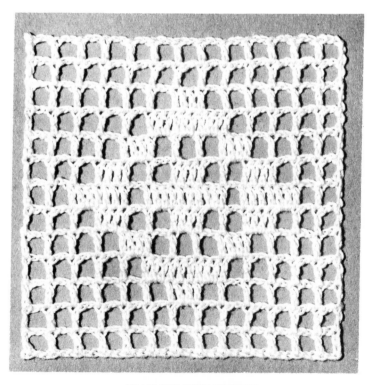

FILET CROCHET SWATCH

151

Materials and Suppliers

The following is a list of manufacturers whose materials were used, or could be substituted, for the projects in this book. As a handy reference when substituting materials, the label name and a brief description is given for each yarn. If you have any problem finding supplies in your area, you can write directly to the manufacturer for information. All materials are nationally distributed and the manufacturers will be able to provide you with names of the stores nearest you that carry their products. Some companies will sell directly to the consumer. This is indicated where applicable.

Supplier:	**Materials:**
American Thread High Ridge Park Stamford, Conn. 06905 *Attn: Design Studio*	Star Embroidery Cotton (6-strand, 9 yd. skeins) Dawn Wool (4-ply, solid colors in 4 oz. skeins, ombre colors in 3½ oz. skeins) Dawn Sayelle (4-ply Orlon acrylic, solid colors in 4 oz. skeins, ombre colors in 3½ oz. skeins) Aunt Lydia's Heavy Rug Yarn (bulky-weight Rayon and cotton blend, 70 yd. and 180 yd. skeins)
C. J. Bates & Son, Inc. Chester, Conn. 06412	Luxite "Bone" Rings (plastic — available in dimestores, craft shops, art-needlework stores, and at the needlework and craft counters of department stores)
Emile Bernat & Sons Co. Uxbridge, Mass. 01569 *Attn: Customer Service*	Carioca (Nylon and acetate blend, light-weight novelty yarn, 1 oz. skeins) Bernat Knitting Worsted (4-ply wool, 4 oz. balls) Berella "4" (4-ply Orlon acrylic, solid and ombre colors in 4 oz. balls) Big Berella Bulky (Orlon and Nylon blend, 4 oz. balls) Quickspun (heavy bulky-weight Acrilan acrylic, 35 yd. skeins)
Bernhard Ulmann Co. 30–20 Thomson Avenue Long Island City, N.Y. 11101 *Attn: Customer Service*	Bucilla Six-Strand Embroidery Floss (cotton, 9 yd. skeins) Bucilla Persian Type Needlepoint and Crewel Wool (3-strand, 40 yd. skeins) Bucilla Tapestry Wool (40 yd. and 100 yd. skeins)

Bernhard Ulmann Co. (cont'd)	Bucilla Paradise (Ban-lon yarn, 1 oz. skeins)
	Bucilla Wool and Shetland Wool (2-ply, 2 oz. balls)
	Bear Brand Winsom (Orlon acrylic, 2 oz. skeins, interchangeable with "Wool and Shetland Wool")
	Bucilla Twin-Pak Knitting Worsted (4-ply wool, solid colors in 4 oz. paks, ombree colors in 3½ oz. paks)
	Bear Brand Twin-Pak Win-Knit (4-ply Orlon acrylic, solid colors in 4 oz. paks, ombree colors in 3½ oz. paks)
	Bucilla Multi-Craft (bulky acrylic, 2 oz. skeins)
Bon Marché 74 Fifth Avenue New York, N.Y. 10011 (*Will sell directly to consumer*)	Chrome frame director's chair
Boye Needle Co. 4343 N. Ravenswood Avenue Chicago, Ill. 60613	Cabone Rings (plastic) — For buying information, see listing for C. J. Bates
Coats & Clark's Sales Corp. 75 Rockefeller Plaza New York, N.Y. 10019	J. & P. Coats Deluxe Embroidery Floss (6-strand cotton, 9 yd. skeins)
	Coats & Clark's Pearl Cotton (size #5, 50 yd. balls)
	J. & P. Coats (Coats & Clark) Knit-Cro-Sheen (cotton, 175 yd. balls)
	Coats & Clark's Speed-Cro-Sheen (cotton, 100 yd. balls)
	Coats & Clark's "Red Heart" Knitting Worsted (4-ply wool, solid colors in 4 oz. skeins, ombre colors in 3½ oz. skeins)
	Coats & Clark's Red Heart Wintuk (4-ply acrylic, solid colors in 4 oz. skeins, ombre colors in 3½ oz. skeins)
	Coat's & Clark's Craft and Rug Yarn (3-ply bulky-weight acrylic, 4 oz. skeins)
Columbia-Minerva Box 500 Robesonia, Pa. 19551	Needlepoint and Crewel Yarn (3-strand wool, 25 yd. pull skeins)
	Lady Handicraft Tapestry Yarn (wool, 40 yd. pull skeins)
	Nantuk Sweater and Afghan Yarn (2-ply Orlon acrylic, 2 oz. skeins)
	Wool 4-Ply (4 oz. skeins)
	Nantuk 4-Ply (Orlon acrylic, solid colors in 4 oz. skeins, ombre colors in 3½ oz. skeins)
	Bulky Nantuk (Orlon acrylic, 75 yd. skeins)
Edgemont Yarn Service (January & Wood Co.) R. R. 2, Box 14 Maysville, Ky. 41056 (*Will sell directly to consumer*)	"Home-Ties" #15 Cable Cord (125 ft. balls)
	"Home-Ties" Indoor Line (45 ft. skeins)
Lily Mills Co. Handweaving Dept. Shelby, N.C. 28150 (*Will sell directly to consumer*)	Lily Embroidery Floss (6-strand cotton, 9 yd. skeins)
	Lily Perle Cotton (size #5, 2 oz. tubes — approx. 263 yds.)
	Lily Double Quick (crochet cotton, 115 yd. skeins)

Reynolds Yarns, Inc.
15 Oser Avenue
Hauppauge, N.Y. 11787
(*Will sell directly to consumer*)
Send orders to:
International Creations
Box 55
Great Neck, Long Island, N.Y. 11023

Reynolds Parfait (Orlon and nylon blend, light-weight novelty yarn, 1 oz. balls)
Reynelle Orlon (4-ply, 4 oz. skeins)
Reynolds Ombre (4-ply Orlon acrylic, 4 oz. skeins)
Reynolds Original Lopi Icelandic Wool (bulky-weight, 3.6 oz. skeins)
Bulky Reynelle (bulky-weight Orlon acrylic, 2 oz. skeins)
Tapis Pingouin (heavy bulky-weight acrylic rug yarn, 1¾ oz. skeins)

Spinnerin Yarn Co., Inc.
230 Fifth Avenue
New York, N.Y. 10001

Spinnerin Tapestry Wool (40 yd. pull skeins)
Marvel Twist Deluxe Knitting Worsted (4-ply wool, 4 oz. skeins)
Germantown Deluxe (4-ply Orlon acrylic, 4 oz. skeins)

William Unger & Co., Inc.
230 Fifth Avenue
New York, N.Y. 10001
(*Will sell directly to consumer*)
Send orders to:
Scandinavian Import Corp.
P.O. Box 347, Madison Square
  Station
New York, N.Y. 10010

Cruise (Nylon and acrylic blend, light-weight novelty yarn, 1$\frac{9}{10}$ oz. balls)
Roly-Poly (3-ply acrylic, 3½ oz. balls)
Cozy (acrylic and wool blend, bulky-weight yarn, 1¾ oz. balls)

Walbead Inc.
38 West 37th Street
New York, N.Y. 10018
(*Will sell directly to consumer —
$5.00 minimum order*)

Wood Beads